Sexual Assault

Sexual Assault

Will I Ever Feel Okay Again?

KAY SCOTT

BETHANY HOUSE PUBLISHERS
Minneapolis, Minnesota 55438

Portions of this book originally appeared in the title *Raped*, by Deborah Roberts, published by The Zondervan Corporation in 1981.

Edited by Judith E. Markham

Published by Bethany House Publishers
A Ministry of Bethany Fellowship, Inc.
11300 Hampshire Avenue South
Minneapolis, Minnesota 55438

Printed in the United States of America

Library of Congress Cataloging-in-Publication Data

Scott, Kay.
    Sexual assault: will I ever feel okay again? / Kay Scott.
       p. cm.
    Rev. ed. of: Raped / Deborah Roberts. ©1981.
    1. Scott, Kay. 2. Rape victims—United States—Biography.
I. Scott, Kay. Raped. II. Title.
HV6561.S38   1993
362'.88'3'092—dc20   93–4939
[B]   CIP
ISBN 1–55661–325–3

To
Robert
and
Carrie and Jeff
and to
every victim of sexual violence
who shared your experience with me.
By what you have taught me, together we give to others.

KAY SCOTT is a writer and homemaker who graduated from Hope College. The story of her recovery from rape was first published in 1981 under the title *Raped*. This edition has been revised and updated with current information on the subject of sexual assault. She has spoken out on television and radio about her experience and has had a one-on-one ministry to survivors of rape. She and her husband have two children and live in Michigan.

Acknowledgments

To Robert

You believed in this book from its inception. Like no one else could, you walked every step of the road with me, offering never-ending support and self-sacrifice. During the writing of both editions you willingly became a sounding board, providing exceptional aid and wise counsel. You faced accompanying adversities with steady strength and perseverance. My best friend, my love, my partner in prayer, for all this book has required of you and will require of you in the years to come, I am deeply grateful.

To Carrie and Jeff

I am truly thankful that without reservation you both offered your support of this project. Thank you for your encouragement, your prayers, and your belief in this ministry. Thank you, too, for the laughter and joy you both bring into our family. I love you more than yesterday and less than tomorrow.

To Rev. Dick Welscott

I am grateful for your mentorship during the writing of the first edition of this book. Many of these pages should be initialed by you, as you provided guidance and insight that contributed to both the seasoning and the substance of the book. Not only did you challenge me and provide feedback and encouragement, but by helping me face even the darkest corners of my life with confidence, you helped me grow yet another set of wings. For all of your help during those two years, thank you.

To Rev. Ron Beyer

Thank you for your sermon, which has touched hearts and changed lives. Including mine. Including yours, I know. We hold a special place in our hearts for David.

I am grateful for the privilege of working with Judith Markham, a proficient editor who is both understanding and sensitive to the plight of the rape victim. Judy, what a joy to have worked with you on both the first and second editions of this book! (Let's do Blimpies.) I also wish to express appreciation to Bethany House Publishers for accepting this project without hesitation, and for patiently waiting as I passed (how many?) deadlines. Special thanks to Carol Johnson.

Candace Walters, you have contributed more to this book than even I know. Thank you for being both a mentor and a friend over the past several years.

I extend special appreciation to Dawn and Steve VanderArk. Thank you for the use of your beautiful log home on the lake, which provided an inspiring setting to capture the vision. You're wonderful!

I gratefully acknowledge the YWCA sexual assault center in Grand Rapids, Michigan, with special thanks to Patti Haist, M.A. This is a much better book because of your expertise. Also, thanks to Argie Holliman.

There are several other people who also reviewed material and offered valuable feedback. Thank you to Rev. LeRoy Koopman for reading portions of the very first draft and for recommending publication. Also, thank you to Scott H. Glass, M.S., M.A., Jim Fongers, M.S.W., C.S.W., Rev. Michael Bos, Tim Jackson, M.A., Th.M., L.P.C., Barb Listing, and Susan Heartwell.

I also wish to express my appreciation to Jan Bast, Brenda Ingersoll, and the word processing department at Miller, Johnson for your technical assistance.

Mark and Carol, thanks for being there, for listening, for caring.

How blessed I am to have special people in my life like Rick and Christi McCollum, my Hope College friends, W.O.R.D. Fellowship, C.B.M.C., and Sunshine friends who supported me with prayers and frequent words of encouragement during the writing of this book.

To Dick and Marge Scott, I am grateful for years of love, care, and support beyond measure.

To the following people who helped in various ways the first time around, please know that the impact of your support has not faded through the years. Thank you to Mary Welscott, Tom Dekker, Bev Zondervan, Pat Buist, Pat Hamilton, Joyce Purdue, Glenn and Phyllis Wissink, and Paul's mom and dad.

To the significant other people not mentioned by name, including relatives, no matter how large or seemingly small a part you played, please accept my deepest gratitude.

Finally, thank you to the many recovering victims of sexual violence who shared your stories with me. You are both the inspiration and the motivation for the second edition of this book.

A Note to the Reader

Some of the names and places have been changed in this otherwise true account to protect the privacy of the individuals involved. Kay Scott is the author's real name, although her maiden name has been changed to honor the request of family members. Since the offender's guilt has not been established by a court of law, it is necessary to protect his privacy.

For ease of reading, the victim has been referred to in the feminine gender. The material provided may also be applicable to male victims of sexual assault.

Many victim advocates now choose to use the term "survivor" to emphasize strength, empowerment, and potential for survival. The author, however, prefers to continue using "recovering [or] recovered victim," to emphasize that those victimized by sexual violence are not responsible for either the crime or the subsequent damage.

Since the focus of this book is emotional and spiritual recovery, it does not address every aspect of sexual assault. Other resources are available to offer education and assistance in areas not covered by this book.

Contents

Introduction

My friend's son had drowned only two days before. He was beautiful. He was vivacious. He was five years old.

As I waited to offer Marcy whatever support I could, I overheard the woman ahead of me say, "Marcy, you know that I know what you're going through." Tears were streaming down her cheeks as she continued, "It was a long time ago, but—"

Marcy completed her statement, "But it comes back hard, doesn't it?" The woman broke down and could not control the flow of tears.

I didn't know this other woman or her situation, but I understood from the conversation that she must have experienced the loss of a loved one, maybe even a child of her own, some years before. She was only trying to help, trying to share in Marcy's grief; instead, her message was that many years later, she still hurt terribly.

I know the pain that comes with the death of a loved one and the pain of rape are not to be compared. They are completely different. Yet something about this incident spoke to me. It has to do with the message I mean to give to you, the reader.

Though my honesty and forthrightness sometimes get me into trouble, here I feel it necessary to tell the whole truth, omitting nothing, not even the sexual adjustment to

15

rape. Sexual violence is horrible, and I must show openly how horrible an experience it is.

But I cannot stop there. You see, the message of this book is the message I wish that woman had been able to convey to my friend, Marcy: *Our God is a big God.* And there is no tragedy so great that each of us, together with God, cannot get through. If we hold on to His promises, we can reach a day when the pain no longer rages and the tears no longer flow.

But even more than that, for those who belong to God there is healing. There is wholeness. There is peace. And there is even joy. For in the rebuilding of our lives we discover the fullness of God's love.

PART ONE

The Story

The story that follows begins in June, 1969. Hitchhikers were a common sight on freeways then. Loaded down with duffle bags and college textbooks, they held up brown cardboard signs marked with their destinations. A minority of people locked their homes in those days, and those who did were often thought to be alarmists.

Sibling to the hippie culture, a new breed of social activism was born in the sixties generation. Young men burned their draft cards, and peace marches cropped up on college campuses across the nation. Compassion for the underprivileged flowed deep, as Elvis's "In the Ghetto" topped the charts. Americans landed on the moon that summer of 1969, the same summer freedom rocked at a concert called Woodstock. This generation had stopped whispering the word "sex." But it had not yet learned to do the same with the word "rape."

1

As our family's two-year-old cranberry Cougar crossed the bridge into the inner-city neighborhood where I would spend my summer, I wondered if our car would make us look like the outsiders we were. I imagined that the people whose lives were so heavily supported by government funds would be driving junkers. Apparently I was wrong. Big black Buicks. Stylish Thunderbirds with the brand-new sequential taillights. How could these people afford such cars? Maybe this neighborhood wasn't so bad after all.

In my narrow mind I had pictured the inner-city living conditions as much worse. I remembered driving past the slums on the south side of Chicago before the Robert Taylor Homes had been built there by the government. Tall, narrow buildings, each a twin to its neighbor, with only a crack of light separating them. From the back there was nothing to view but stairs and banisters . . . five stories of laundry hanging from pulley clotheslines . . . tricycles on six-foot by three-foot porches. Row after row of identical houses with only an occasional tree to break up the cement, the brick— the hard surfaces that so adequately symbolized the hardness of the residents' lives.

It was years ago that I, as a young child, had seen those slums, but ever since, that was how I had pictured inner-city neighborhoods. Now I had grown and changed. So had the city.

I snapped back to reality and tried to take in all my surroundings. My immediate impression was that it wasn't so bad. The area didn't look too rough. As we turned the corner onto Barclay Street, I could see more of the projects, three-story brick buildings with windows that opened out. They looked institutional but not run-down, at least not from the outside. We turned another corner, stopping on Griswold Street. There it was! 1802. The second house from the corner. My father parked in the only space left on the street, and I was the first one out of the car. My mother, father, and younger sister followed.

The three boys walking toward us on the sidewalk couldn't have been more than nine years old, yet there was something about them that made me uncomfortable. Something was missing . . . a skateboard, a baseball glove, a swimming suit rolled up in a towel . . . they carried nothing. Their walk was a worldly wise saunter, as if their childhood had already been spent. I wondered if our hubcaps would be there when we returned.

Suddenly I was anxious to see a familiar face in this place. As we approached Reverend Quillan's house, I became aware of a churning in my stomach. My excitement had turned to nervousness. Would I do a good job here? What would my roommate be like? What would this job be like? What would I be doing while I was here? What did the people in my comfortable suburb mean when they said, "It will be a good experience for you. . . . You'll see what the world is really like"? Added to my nervousness was impatience. I wanted to experience it all at once.

There was a bright yellow smiley-face sign above Reverend Quillan's door that read, "Smile, God loves you." It made me feel better, but not comfortable. I would like it here. I knew I would. God had led me here for the summer. It couldn't be any other way.

It had been only two months since I had decided to do

something more meaningful than clerk in a jewelry store for another summer. On my college campus was a small meditation chapel that had become a haven for me—a place for peace and quiet and prayer. I had gone there one afternoon to ask God to use my summer for His service. On my way back to the dorm, I had picked up the college bulletin and an ad had caught my eye:

NEEDED: Two college students to work in urban church for ten weeks this summer. Applications available in chaplain's office.

I hadn't expected God's answer quite so immediately, but responding to an overwhelming, compelling feeling, I went directly to the chaplain's office. I filled out the forms and waited to be called, all the while praying that, if it was within God's will, I might be chosen.

Reverend Quillan, the minister at the inner-city church, came to campus and interviewed twenty-five students, myself included. It all happened so fast that I was chosen before I had even told my parents I had applied for the job.

Deanna was to be my roommate for the summer. Although we both attended the same college, we had not met. It would be fun getting to know Deanna as we worked together. We were going to share Jesus with the people in the city. I had seen the faces before of those who had accepted Christ into their lives. I couldn't wait to see that again. The people there needed Him so much. It would be a wonderful summer. I just knew it!

———

The entrance to our attic apartment was in the back of the tall, narrow, red brick house where Reverend Quillan and his family lived. Deanna and I had to climb five flights of wooden stairs to reach the top of the three-story building. The first door led into the rough, unfinished outer attic. The second opened into our kitchen where we had an old chrome table, a small refrigerator, and a hot plate. Since we had no plumbing in the kitchen, we washed our dishes in the large footed bathtub and rinsed them in the bathroom sink. We managed without kitchen cupboards, too, keeping everything from tomato soup to laundry detergent on three rows of shelves in a closet we called our pantry.

Our two single beds barely fit under the slant of the roof in the bedroom. A narrow aisle between them allowed us to get to the table with the old black telephone on it or to the window.

Looking out the large window was like sitting on top of the city street. A small tree only partially blocked the view of the concrete below. We could watch the shifts change at strange hours of the day and night at the laundry across the street. It was the first time I had seen people going to work in T-shirts and cutoff jeans. My father had always worn a suit, a tie, and a freshly pressed shirt to his teaching job. My mother, also a teacher, dressed smartly and tastefully in dresses or skirts and blouses. Here, dirty and sweaty men and women came out of the prisonlike, block-long brick building. I was never aware of a parking lot for the laundry. Probably because most of the people were from the neighborhood. They walked to and from their jobs each day, carrying their black lunch boxes or brown paper sacks.

Usually at the end of a shift a small group of men would gather on the concrete outside the building. They would pause for a cigarette, carrying on loud conversations before heading to their various apartments or row houses. But most of the people who left were women dressed in work shirts and pants. I wondered where their children were while they worked long hours at their factory jobs. We discovered later that many of them were left to fend for themselves. Tommy was one of these children, and I remember vividly the day we met him.

Deanna and I had been out recruiting door-to-door for Project Head Start. We had climbed to the third floor of one of the apartment buildings, and it was my turn to knock on the door. I could hear a TV inside, but no one answered. I knocked harder. The door pushed open ever so slowly, only a crack. Two puppylike brown eyes, nearly covered by long black curls, peered out at us. At first I couldn't tell if it was a boy or a girl.

"Hello there. My name is Kay, and this is Deanna. What's your name?"

No answer.

"Is your mother home?"

Still no answer.

I turned to Deanna. "Maybe he doesn't speak English."

"Habla español?"

He just stared. The longer he stared, the more frustrated I became.

"That's okay. Thank you anyway."

"Let's try this door," Deanna suggested, pointing to the apartment just across the hall. An elderly lady answered my knock.

"Hi. We're recruiting for Head Start. We're looking for four- and five-year-olds. Do you know if there are any living in this building? We haven't been able to find anybody at home."

"Uh, don't know. Don't know the folks here."

"Do you happen to know the people across the hall?"

"Some."

"Is there more than one child living there?"

"Nope. Jest Tommy."

"Do you know how old Tommy is?"

"He's eight. But his mom's not here. She's in the hospital. Goin' on two weeks now."

"Oh, I see. What about his father?"

"Never can tell where he's at. Ain't been seen in six months."

"Tommy's all by himself now, then?"

"Yeah, but I look after him when I can."

"Oh, that's very nice of you. Let's see . . . if he's eight, he must be in second or third grade, then?"

"Oh, no. Tommy don't go to school. His mom don't send him."

"Oh, I don't mean in the summer—"

"No. He ain't never been."

"He's never been to school?"

"That's right. His mom don't send him, and the school's never got him. Prob'ly don't know he's here."

"Could you please tell me Tommy's last name?"

"Pierce."

"Thank you. You've been very helpful."

I couldn't believe it! An eight-year-old who had never been to school . . . and living all alone! We would give his name to Reverend Quillan. He would find a way to help Tommy.

Door-to-door recruiting for Head Start and Project Friendly Town taught us a lot about the people in the projects. We were five miles from Lake Michigan, yet many of the kids had never been to the beach. Much of their life was broken glass and asphalt playgrounds.

Even though drugs were available to anyone who wanted them, alcoholism was a much bigger problem. Nearly all the teenagers drank beer and were usually drunk on the weekends. I wasn't used to that. My family didn't drink at all, and the suburban teenagers I knew who drank were usually discreet about it. Here everything was out in the open—right on the street!

One afternoon when Deanna and I were talking with some of the kids in the courtyard of an apartment building, a guy came up to me and said, "Want a sip of my beer?"

"No, thanks."

"Whatsa matter? Somethin' wrong wit' my beer?"

"Nope. I just don't drink beer."

"You don't drink beer?" He grabbed me by the arm. "Have a sip or I'll pour it over your head."

I just looked up at him and laughed, "Go ahead. I hear beer shampoos are great for your hair!"

Fortunately, for my sake, he decided not to do it. Laughing about it had eased the tension. But the whole drinking problem continued to bother me for the duration of my stay in the city.

One of our objectives for the summer was to organize activities to keep the kids off the streets and out of trouble. Our storefront coffeehouse helped to serve that purpose. The kids could come there several nights a week and play cards, listen to their own kind of music, drink soda pop, and just get together for a good time without the drugs, the beer, or the police breathing down their necks. On the street they could be arrested for gathering in groups of more than five. At the coffeehouse they could freely mix and share their lives with each other and with us. We got to know a few of them quite well. Rudy is one I will never forget.

"I ain't never been in no po-lice station," he would boast.

"Aw, Rudy, you have so. Everybody been one time or 'nother."

"I ain't neither."

"You never been down fer nothin'? You lie, guy. I knows you lie."

"All right. All right, man. I been there. Ta register ma bike, man. But I ain't been there no time else."

The other kids would jeer and give him a hard time, but they respected Rudy more than any other kid on the streets. He was level-headed and somehow managed to keep out of trouble. Because he was such a good influence on the others, he was a big help to us in the coffeehouse.

We hoped to attract Rudy and some of the other teen-agers to come on Sundays as well, when our storefront coffeehouse became our place of worship. On a good Sunday we would have twenty-five to thirty people there. Coming from a suburban church of four hundred families, that didn't seem like much of a church to me at first. But I quickly learned that even though the numbers were few, God was working and changing lives. Ever so slowly, growth was taking place. I acquired a great deal of respect for Reverend Quillan for sticking by those people the four years he had already been there. "Rev," as he was affectionately known, was a family man, the father of three young children. He was a simple man, though not in the least ordinary. He held a strong vision for the future of this inner-city church. Watching the people in the neighborhood struggle through their daily lives, he worked to bring them meaning and hope through the message of Christ. It was a dream we all shared for the people in the projects. Yet it was a goal that would not be quickly or easily realized.

2

Deanna and I spent the first four weeks in the city recruiting for Project Head Start and Project Friendly Town, tutoring at the Boys' Club, making plans for a backyard school, participating in Sunday worship, helping to run the coffeehouse, and in general trying to get to know the neighborhood and the people in it.

Our fifth week was spent away from the city as counselors at Camp Manitoqua, our denomination's church camp. Sometime later in the summer some of the kids from the projects would spend a week there, but this time just Deanna and I went.

We were given two different cabins for the week. All ten of the girls in my cabin were in junior high school, which, I discovered, was an obnoxious age. But in six short days I grew to love each one of them dearly. On the last day of camp I felt as if I was leaving my own family. I was. Every single one of them had made a personal commitment to Christ the night before. We were family.

And yet I was anxious to get back to my job in the city. After all, that was what this summer was all about. Rev had sent the two of us to camp only because there had been a shortage of counselors for that particular week. My real job was in the projects, and I was ready to return.

Deanna looked tired the morning we left. Even at the

young age of nineteen, five or six hours of sleep a night had not been nearly enough for either of us. Since the night before had been the Fourth of July as well as the last night at camp, we had all been up until the "wee hours" laughing, singing, and celebrating in true holiday spirit.

It wasn't until the tearful good-byes had been said and all the campers had gone that Rev arrived to pick us up in the church van. The ride back to the city was long, and by the time we got to our apartment, the week's activities had caught up with us. Exhaustion hit. At 11:30 in the morning Deanna and I were ready for a good night's sleep, but a nap would have to do.

After we had been asleep nearly four-and-a-half hours, the alarm buzzed. Groggy and barely functioning, I managed to find the ten-minute delay button. I slammed my palm down on top of it, silencing the annoying sound. When it rang the second time, I was awake enough to remember that we were back in the city and had work to do. Besides, I was hungry—reason enough to get up.

Deanna was still sound asleep.

"Deanna."

No reply.

"Deanna, get up."

"Huh?"

"Get up. We have to go shopping."

"Shopping? Oh, yeah. Right. Shopping? What for?"

Since we had been gone for a week, we had no food in the apartment. It was a short walk to the neighborhood grocery store, and on our way back we began to plan the week ahead of us. Only one thing had to be taken care of yet that day. Rev had prepared some fliers to inform the people in the projects that the church was moving to the Boys' Club a block away. The storefront we had been renting was to be demolished to make room for a parking lot. The move was only temporary, until we could locate another place for the church and the coffeehouse ministry, but since it was to go into effect the next day, we had to get word to the people right away.

Delivering the notices would only take an hour or so,

but as Deanna and I set out for the projects, we were both aware that it was quickly becoming Saturday night on the streets of Chicago. It was chilly for the first week in July, and I had put on blue jeans, a sweatshirt, and my college windbreaker.

The small children were still out, and it was not dark yet, but it soon would be. If we stayed together, we would not get finished until after dark, so we decided to split up. I took the row houses on the left side of Griswold Street, and Deanna took the three-story apartments on the right side of the street. After I finished on my side, I would cross over and start working my way back until we met. We would be finished in no time.

After I had put the notices in several mailboxes, I stopped on the sidewalk to look back. I didn't see Deanna at first, but in a few seconds she appeared. She waved. Apparently she had been watching for me, too. I waved back. After that I picked up the pace. I would show her how fast I could get my part of the job done.

Feeling confident and in good spirits, I chatted with some of the children along the way. When I came to the end of the street, I noticed a group of guys loitering on the corner, four or five of them. I hadn't seen Deanna for a while and an uneasiness set in, but not enough to squelch my enthusiasm. When I got to the last row house, I realized that the guys were standing in front of the mailbox. I didn't recognize any of them, but I didn't want to insult them by not going to their house. They had all turned and were staring at me, probably wondering what I was handing out.

I had to pass so close to them that I felt I had to say something, especially since they were all staring at me. So I said, "Hi!" and handed a flier to the nearest one. He grabbed my arm and said, "Want to come to my party?" I could smell the beer on his breath. I pulled my arm back with a curt, "No, thank you," crossed the street, and entered the door of the first apartment building.

I heard something behind me. Someone had followed me into the entryway of the apartment building. It was the guy who had grabbed my arm, and he was between me and the door I had just come through—the only way out. It was only five feet away, but out of reach. I put the notices into the mailboxes with a rhythm that matched the rapid tempo of my heartbeat, then turned to leave as quickly as possible.

"Where you goin'?"

"I'm leaving. I'm all done here. Excuse me." I tried to move past him, but he pushed me up against the wall.

"How about goin' to my party, huh?"

"Sorry. I've got work to do." Funny. There had been several guys standing outside, but no girls. I hadn't heard any music. No real signs of a party. What did he want?

The answer to this question came suddenly. He threw me up against the wall a second time and stuck his dirty hands up inside my sweatshirt. He grabbed my bra, yanking it up. At the instant his hands touched my breasts, I shrank from the inside out and struggled to get past him to the door. I made it to the door and could have made it out if I could have just pushed the door open, but the door had to be opened toward me, and he was right there behind me.

He grabbed me and pushed me around, blocking my only escape route. I knew I was in trouble. Where was Deanna? If I could just stall him. She would be coming soon. He reached for his back pocket and threatened, "Now, I don't want to hurt you." I knew he had a knife. Everyone on these streets carried knives. I could see him clearly now. He had a pockmarked complexion and short, fuzzy hair. But it was his piercing eyes that frightened me most. I had never seen such a repulsive, wicked expression of power.

I had no doubts now. I knew what he was after.

"Would it matter to you if I told you I had syphilis? I do, you know." Anything to stall him.

"Who's your boyfriend?"

Maybe this was my chance. "He's a Black Spider." I knew the Black Spiders were a gang from outside the neighborhood. Was that enough to scare him off? Or would it just encourage him all the more?

"Does he know Joe?"

"Of course." *Who's Joe?* How long could I carry this bluff? Had I already blown it? *Dear Lord, help me.*

With one rough tug he unzipped my jeans. "I'm having my period," I pleaded. It didn't seem to matter to him.

I had inched away from the wall, and he threw me up against it again. And again I tried to get away, but couldn't get past him. I could fake fainting. It wouldn't be too tough to fake. I was beginning to feel very weak. *Dear Lord, help me faint. Get me out of this, please, God.* My body became totally limp, and I slumped to the floor.

No! O God! No! Make him leave me alone! He had picked up my feet and was dragging me away, away from the door, away from the street, down the stairs that led to the basement. *O God, who can help me now?* Still limp, I tried to raise my head just enough to keep it from bouncing against the hard steps. I prayed again. *Lord, please spare me this. Let me live. . . . I know. . . . he thinks I've passed out. When we get to the bottom and he lets go of my legs, I'll jump up and startle him enough to break away and make a run for it.*

As I hit the bottom step, I leaped to my feet, but he already had a tight grip on me. I felt the burn of captivity singe through my arm, then through my entire body. He reached for his blade again. "I don't want to hurt you," he said, not with compassion, but with a life-threatening sting. He wrenched my hand from the banister, shoving me to the basement floor. Where was Deanna? *What if she doesn't find me down here? What if she goes home without me?*

The floor was filthy. I could feel it all around me. The stench of urine permeated the air.

"Take off your pants."

I couldn't move.

He yanked off one leg of my jeans . . . then my under-pants. I couldn't watch. My eyes closed, I could hear him loosen his belt and remove his pants. He pushed my feet up so that my knees were in the air.

That moment . . . that single moment of pain. No, the word "pain" cannot touch it. There is no word to describe it. It cannot be compared to a burn or a gunshot wound or a broken bone or a knife piercing the body. It's a pain like no other. It's a pain that kills. It kills every breath of life within. All energy . . . all will to resist . . . gone . . . dead.

Defeated. *I can't move. I'm not me. I'm not here. I am dead. I am nothing. I am . . . no longer.*

That moment in time . . . no, there was no moment. There was no time. There was nothing but evil. *My God, where are you? My God, my God. Where are you? Evil crushes me. Grinds me into dust. Oh, my God. I can't bear it. I can't bear it. Why have you left me? Oh, God, where are you? Help me. Someone. Please help me.*

"You're a virgin," he mocked.

"Yes." A whisper was all I could get out.

The sound of the door opening startled me. Someone was at the top of the stairs, only a few steps away. His hand smothered my mouth. I thought he would break my jaw. *Oh, my God . . . I don't want anyone to see me like this. Please, God, let this person help, but don't let anyone see.*

"Kay, are you down there?" Thank God. It was Deanna.

He fumbled for his back pocket again. Before he released my mouth, he whispered intensely, with his face inches from mine, "Get rid of her. I know where you live."

"Yeah, Deanna . . . go . . . on ahead."

There was a pause. Then the sound of the door opening and . . . closing. She had left. With her went any particle of strength I had left. What was I to do now?

Savagely he continued ramming himself into me. After a few minutes had passed, the door opened again.

"Kay?"

"Deanna?"

"Get rid of her or I'll get her, too!" he hissed.

What could I say to alert her without angering him into killing me? *Lord, help.*

"Should I go back to the place?" she asked before I could think of anything to say.

"Yes, I think that would be a good idea." *Oh, Lord. What place?* What did she mean? Did she sense my danger? Was she going to get Rev or was she just going home? I had to believe she was going for help. I had to.

Even after those interruptions, he kept forcing himself into me. Then he stopped.

"I'm taking you to my party." Terror struck. *No! His*

friends! They'll get me, too! No! If we left, Deanna would never find me. There were hundreds of apartments on this block. I had to stall. He stood up, pulling his pants on.

"Get up!" He seemed nervous now and kept looking toward the top of the stairs. Pulling up his zipper, he yelled at me again. "Hurry up! You're going to my party."

I sat up very slowly, delaying as much as I dared. Before my clothes were fully adjusted, he grabbed my arm and dragged me behind him up the stairs. I knew I had to try to break loose when we got on the street. It was my only chance.

"Don't forget, we all know where you live," he threatened again as we reached the entryway. Just then the door opened. It was Rev. I felt a surge of relief and a new terror all at the same time. What if his friends were still out there? What if they hurt Rev, too? They could kill us both!

I deliberately fastened my belt so that Rev could see, hoping that would reveal to him what had happened.

"What were you doing down there?" Rev demanded. The magnitude of his voice did not match the small, almost frail frame of his body. Rev was street tough, even though his build did not reflect that fact.

Somehow my captor managed to scream in my ear at a whisper's pitch, "I want him to see you kiss me. Tell him you're my girlfriend or I'll get you. My friends know where to find you." He was reaching for his knife again.

When we got out on the street, I could see the church van. Deanna was in it. It was an object of safety, and I was not far from it. Would this horrid ordeal finally end? The other guys were not in sight, but they could be anywhere . . . watching. I was positive they were.

He still gripped my arm tightly. "I gotta talk ta my girl," he said to Rev, pulling me a few feet away so that we were still in plain sight, but out of normal voice range. Rev watched intently, looking angry but confused.

"Do it. Kiss me. Now." His mouth attacked mine, and I felt my lips being forced open by his tongue. Repulsed by this vulgar act, I wanted to back away, but he had his arms strapped tight to my back.

"Show the Rev this was all your idea," he insisted. Afraid of what he might do if I didn't, I put my arms around him. In front of Rev, in front of Deanna, in front of the whole world. Although I was clothed, I was naked and all could see.

He stopped only long enough to threaten me again. "Don't you call the pigs, you hear?" He crammed the words into my ear as he tightened his grip.

"Again, baby." He forced his awful kiss on me again.

Now Rev was walking toward us. "Let go of her. Kay, get in the van." Rev was taking control of the situation.

I felt his grip loosen . . . I was released.

"Are you all right?" Rev asked gently as I walked by him.

I nodded. I could not find words to break through the wall of my humiliation. As I reached the van, I could hear Rev asking his name. "Joe Nemeth," was the reply.

I watched from the van as the two of them stood face-to-face. The guy kept reaching for his back pocket, and I knew he was threatening Rev too. I searched the street outside the van with my eyes and ears, fearful that his friends were still around. Deanna tried to start up a conversation.

"I've never seen him before . . . what are they talking about?" she asked. I couldn't respond. I was terrified for Rev.

A moment later Rev was walking back to the van, and the attacker headed across the street to the row house where I had first seen him. He ducked around the building and was gone. It was over. We were all safe. I pulled air into my lungs and let it out again. It hurt. My entire body ached.

As Rev climbed into the van, Deanna turned toward me and asked, "Do you want to go to the clinic?"

Did she know what had happened in there? Did Rev? They must. I was relieved. It meant I didn't have to tell them.

As we were sitting there in the van, a police car drove up and parked behind us. Two policemen got out and walked directly into the entryway of the building where I had just been. Someone had called the police! Rev said he hadn't called them. Deanna hadn't called them. Who had?

Who? Within moments they came back out and stopped to talk to some little kids playing on the sidewalk. There were no adults in sight. Who had called them? Someone must have seen or heard something!

Rev must have sensed my fear when I saw the police. Maybe he had heard the last threat.

"Whether you go to the clinic or not is up to you, Kay," he said. "But you should know that if you go there, they'll automatically call the police."

Although I was still frightened for all our lives, the threats had begun to lose some of their power over me now that he was out of sight. But I couldn't talk. Not yet. Not to the police. Not to anyone. I was numb. I couldn't move. I ached. From deep inside a message pulsated through me. *You have to talk to the police.* But get out of the van? Back onto that street where that guy and his friends could see me talking to them? No. I would go to the clinic. The police would be called. I would talk to them. But later. *Please get me away from here. Take me anywhere. Just get me out of here. Take me away. Please.*

"Do you want me to take you to the clinic?" Rev asked.

It was all I could do to respond with one word . . ."Yes."

3

Deanna went into the clinic with me while Rev parked the van. But as soon as I entered the waiting room, I began to wonder what I was doing there. I had never been a patient in a hospital before. Hospitals had always given me the creeps, especially emergency wards. . . . Why was I here? I had no broken bones. As far as the receptionist could tell, I was just fine.

"Yes, may I help you?"

"I need to see a doctor."

"What is this for?"

"I just . . . need to see a doctor."

"I'm sorry, but I have to know what this is for."

"I was raped."

The words fell to the pit of my stomach like dead weights. Hearing myself speak those three words was . . . that disgusting four-letter word was me. *Rape. Me. Oh, God, how could this awful thing happen? How could it happen to me? I don't believe it.*

"Right this way, please."

I was taken to a small examining room and handed a white paper gown. "Take all your clothes off, please. The doctor will be in to see you shortly."

All my clothes? Everything? Oh, please, couldn't I just leave my underpants on?

35

It was so cold in there. Cotton balls in a jar. Tongue depressors in a taller glass jar. Gauze. *What am I doing here? I don't need any of this stuff. . . . Somebody get me out of here. Take me home. The lights are so bright.*

As I heard the doorknob turn, my heart pounded. A doctor and nurse entered.

"Lie down, please, and put your feet in the stirrups."

He walked around to the side of the table and lifted the paper gown. His cold hands pressed against my breast. A swelling scream from deep inside wanted to burst out of me. *Don't touch me! Can't you see I'm okay? You don't have to touch me! Get your hands off me! Oh, God, get me off this table! I'm trapped. I can't move. Get away from me.*

"Since you are still having your period," the doctor said, "the chances of your getting pregnant are pretty slim."

Pregnant! I could be pregnant!

"In two weeks I want you to go to your regular doctor. He'll need to do a test for venereal disease."

It hadn't occurred to me that *he* might have had a venereal disease.

"Have you ever had a pelvic exam before?"

"No."

"Well, just relax."

Relax! Relax? Oh, God. Rape. Pregnant. Venereal disease. Get your fingers out of me. It's my body. Let me go. Don't you touch me! Leave me alone! Oh, God, I can't bear this! Help me. Somebody.

Although I felt like a living volcano with an eruption brewing on the inside, to the doctors and nurses I must have appeared extremely calm. I spoke quietly and only when necessary to answer questions. My thoughts and emotions were so jumbled that I began to lose touch with reality. I felt myself giving in, as if a part of life had left me. That part of me that wanted to fight back—to resist all that was happening to me—left me. Powerless. I was not a part of what was going on. It was all happening to me . . . without me.

Two policemen were brought into the examining room, the same two we had seen at the apartment building. They must have followed us to the clinic. As they asked their probing questions, I answered them calmly. I sat on the examining table naked, covered only by a thin, gaping paper gown. It never occurred to me that I could have refused to talk to them. It never occurred to me that I could have asked to get dressed before talking to them. I had lost all control over my own welfare.

"Your name is Kayleen Marston?"

"Yes."

"Is that spelled K-a-y-l-e-e-n M-a-r-s-t-o-n?"

"Yes, but I go by Kay."

"How old are you?"

"Nineteen."

"Your address?"

"Which one?"

"You have more than one?"

"I'm just living here in the city for the summer."

"Well, we better have both."

I told them what they wanted to know.

"What time did this happen?"

"I don't know."

"Can you give us an approximate time?"

"About forty-five minutes ago."

"About 7:30 then?"

"I guess so."

"Can you tell us what happened?"

"We were delivering—"

"Who's we?"

"Deanna and I."

He turned to his partner. "That's the black girl in the lobby . . . go on."

"We were delivering some notices to tell the people that church services would be moved to the Boys' Club tomorrow . . . He followed me across the street into the apartment building."

"Who's he? Do you know him?"

"No."

"You don't know his name, then?"

"No. Yes. He said it was Joe. Joe Nemeth or something like that."

"Joe Namath?" They both laughed. "Do you know who Joe Namath is?"

"No."

"He's a football player for the New York Jets."

I was still in shock. I felt nothing. It wouldn't be until much later, when I recalled their questions and their laughter, that I would suffer further humiliation and embarrassment.

"Go on."

"I couldn't get out the door."

"What door?"

"The door to the apartment building."

"You were inside the building?"

"Yes. Just inside."

"And he was, too?"

"Yes. He followed me in."

"Deanna was with you?"

"No, we had split up."

"What happened next?"

"He slammed me up against the wall. He put his hands up . . . my shirt."

"Go on."

"I told him I had VD. I tried to faint. He dragged me down the stairs."

"Go on."

"He raped me."

"Where were you? In the basement?"

"Yes, but just at the bottom of the stairs."

"Did you take your own clothes off?"

"No. He told me to, but I didn't."

"He took your clothes off then?"

"Just my pants."

"Did he have a gun?"

"No."

"Any weapon?"

"A knife."

"He pulled it on you?"

"No."

"You didn't see it?"

"No. But he kept reaching for it in his back pocket. He said he didn't want to hurt me."

"He threatened you?"

"Yes."

"What else did he say?"

"He said he knew where I lived. He said he'd get me if I didn't say I was his girlfriend."

"Did he climax?"

"Uh, what do you mean?"

"Are you a . . . uh, were you a virgin?"

"Yes."

He turned to his partner. "She would have known if he had."

"He didn't get any pleasure out of it, if that's what you mean. He wasn't finished with me. He was going to take me to his party."

"What party?"

"At least he said he was having a party. Some of his friends were across the street waiting for him."

"So did he take you across the street to his party?"

"No. Rev came."

"Oh, yeah, the minister. Did you climax . . . uh, have an orgasm?"

"No."

"Have you had intercourse with anyone else today?"

"No."

"Oh, yeah, you said you were a virgin. You understand we have to ask these questions. Uh, could you identify this guy?"

"I don't know."

"Was he black?"

"No."

"Chicano?"

"No, white."

"How tall?"

"Just a little taller than me."

"How tall are you?"

"Five-seven."

"Okay, say five-ten, then?"

"I guess so."

"Hair color?"

"Brown. And curly."

"How much did he weigh?"

"I don't know. He was sort of skinny."

"Any scars or marks on him?"

"I don't think so."

"Did you scratch him?"

"No."

"Did you kick or bite him?"

"No."

He turned again to his partner. "These do-gooders who come here think they're gonna change this place. They're just not tough enough. Some of them get raped three or four times before they finally leave."

Then he turned back to me. "What makes you so calm, anyway?"

"I had help." What I meant was that I had prayed throughout the rape and God had been helping me. But at that moment I didn't really care whether they understood what I meant. They didn't ask, and I didn't try to explain.

God truly had helped me through it. I had survived the attack, and I was thankful that Rev had not brought in a bloody, screaming, hysterical, half-dead victim, which was what the policemen expected to see. By the time they began their questioning, I felt nothing. What they perceived as calmness was actually a numbing quietude brought on by shock. Unfortunately, this would make my case all the more difficult to prove in court.

———

A lot of what took place immediately after the police questioning is buried forever. I don't remember getting dressed or leaving the hospital. I don't remember going back to our apartment, to Rev's house. I can only vaguely recall riding home from the city that same night to tell my parents what had happened. I do remember, though, a piece of conversation that Rev and I had on that trip home.

"Do you think you'll come back?" he asked.

"I . . . don't know." Silence prevailed as I let my thoughts work their way through. "I want to . . . I think. I don't know what my parents will say."

"I called them to tell them I was bringing you home. I just told them you weren't feeling well."

"Oh. What if they don't want me to come back? What about Deanna? Do you think she would stay? By herself?"

"I don't know."

It was after midnight by the time we got to my home. I remember the look on both of my parents' faces when we walked in; they knew something was very wrong. It was Rev who actually told them.

"I wanted to bring her home so you could see that she's okay. Kay was . . . raped tonight."

My mother's gasp drew my eyes from the floor to her face. I wished I hadn't looked at her at that moment. In my mind, I can still see her expression of shock and horror.

I don't remember any more of the conversation that took place between my parents and Rev. I remember that my father saw Rev to the door and thanked him for bringing me home, but the rest is lost. I couldn't have remembered it the next day. The shock erased it all.

"We should write it all down, all the details," my father said after Rev left.

"What?" Exhaustion had set in. I just wanted to go to bed.

"Do you remember when I had that bad car accident? It took six years for that to get to court. Then I had to recall every detail—what I was wearing, exactly what moment I put my foot on the brakes, everything. Better to write it down while it's still fresh in your mind."

At that moment, it seemed like the most horrible thing my father had ever asked me to do. Cruel and heartless. But I was too numb to argue. After my mother went to bed, my father and I stayed up several more hours. He asked the questions and wrote down everything I said as I let him draw it all out of me. It was five in the morning before we finished.

Later, I was grateful that it had been written down. My father's notes were much more detailed than the police report. Later, when I went to court, I didn't have to go through the anguish of trying to remember all that had happened. It was all down on paper. I would read it over and over to refresh my memory until the details became embedded in my mind.

But telling everything to my father was much more difficult than telling the police. I had never before shared the private aspects of my life with him. Describing the intimate details of what had happened left me feeling naked in front of him. I would have to tell my story many times, but that time was the most difficult.

4

Because I was still in shock, little that happened during the next few days is in my conscious memory. Somehow I got from Saturday, July fifth, the day of the rape, to the following Thursday, July tenth. It was to have been my day off, and Bob was coming to see me. Maybe that was why it was the first day I remembered.

My parents suggested that I stay upstairs for a few minutes after he arrived. They would explain to him that I had been a witness to a crime and was still a bit shaken so that I might not seem quite myself. They would also ask him not to question me about it.

It seemed somewhat awkward, but I did agree to it. And it did seem to relieve some of the pressure I felt. Even though Bob and I had only been dating for four months, I knew I had to tell him that I had been raped—and soon. But I wasn't quite sure how he would react or when the time would be right. My parents' plan gave me temporary escape. I was free to enjoy the day with Bob, free to feel more like myself again . . . or so I thought.

We had planned to spend the day in downtown Chicago at a couple of museums. As we were putting together our picnic lunch, Bob suggested that we save the Museum of Science and Industry for the afternoon and go to the aquarium first. We could have our lunch on the lawn at the aquarium, which is exactly what we did.

It was a beautiful day. The sun was warm, and Lake Michigan looked so inviting. The aquarium was located on a point extending out into the lake, so we could watch the kids playing on the beach as we sat on the lawn eating our tuna sandwiches and chips. It had been a pleasant morning. Museums had never interested me much before, but now I was with Bob and away from the trauma of the rape, free to enjoy. Maybe somehow everything would be all right again.

As we walked hand in hand across the parking lot to the car, I was stunned. There, driving toward us, were my parents. At first anger hit me. What were they doing, checking up on us? Were they following us? How had they found us in this city of three million people? And then, almost as suddenly, fear struck. No, they weren't here to check up on us. They were here to get me. The police must have found the guy who had raped me.

Bob had spotted them, too. "What are *they* doing here?" he asked.

"I'm not sure. I'll see what they want."

I left Bob at his car and walked over to where my parents had stopped, a short distance away. As I leaned down to the window on the passenger side, my mother said, "We're sorry to interrupt your day. Looks like you've been having a good time."

"Yeah. What's up? How did you find us?"

"You mentioned you might stop here for lunch. . . . The police picked him up. He's being held at the precinct station. We had to come and get you because they can only hold him for a few hours. They want you to identify him."

Oh, no. I don't want to see him again . . . please.

"How did they find him?" I asked.

"Well, the policeman who called us said Reverend Quillan saw him on the street and called them. They picked him up right away."

Reality forced itself on me. We were to follow my parents to the precinct station, but Bob still had no idea what was going on. I walked back to him, trying to figure out what to say.

"Bob, I'm sorry, but we have to skip the other museum."

"That's okay. What's wrong?"

"I have to go to a police station to identify someone. I don't know where it is, but we can follow my parents."

That was all I said, and Bob asked no questions. It was all I could do to keep up a superficial conversation on the way to the station. My thoughts were tearing me apart. I would have to see *him* again, face-to-face. *Maybe it's not him. Maybe they got the wrong guy. What if I'm not sure it's him?*

My father and I went into the big stone building, leaving Bob and my mother sitting out in my parents' car. We were taken to a back room and were told that I would be looking through a screen through which I could see the suspect, but he would not be able to see me. As I waited for him to be brought into the room, the tension built inside me. When I saw him enter the room, my body became hot all over and I could actually feel the color drain from my face. I had lost all movement, all life. Somehow, I managed to nod my head to the policeman. I could not utter a sound. It was him. There was no doubt.

Although his eyes never met mine, even through the impenetrable mesh I was stricken with fear that he could see me. All his threats came back to me now. He was only a few feet away. He could reach out and touch me. Only the screen separated us. It didn't matter that I was standing in a police station with protection all around me. There had been people on the street only a few yards away from where he had raped me. No one had prevented that. Suddenly it was as if only he and I were there. My terror incapacitated me. Only after he was taken out of my sight did I regain control.

I don't remember how I got from there to the next room. I didn't pass out, but I was in such a state of shock that much of my own physical movement took place without any conscious knowledge on my part. When I returned to reality, I was seated in a larger room that had many backless benches in it—some sort of briefing or meeting room for the policemen.

"Would you like a glass of water?" I looked up. Standing

in front of me, holding out a glass of cold water, was an officer I had not seen before.

"Thank you." I was extremely grateful for his thoughtfulness. It was only a small kindness, but it was as if someone had lit a candle for me in a huge, vast, dark room. The blackness had been pierced. I was beginning to see again. I was regaining control. I could function now.

In order for the police to hold the assailant, I had to sign a formal complaint, which meant going over all the details again. I also had to decide whether I would prosecute. This decision was all the more difficult to make because of the horror of seeing him again. The idea of coming face-to-face with him in court was unbearable. And what of all those threats? If I prosecuted, he would find out all about me and how to get me.

Maybe it was the policeman's assurances that this guy was as scared as I was, maybe it was the fear that people wouldn't believe me if I backed out now, or maybe it was the scratching for survival from deep inside that spoke to me saying, *Press on. Do something. If you stop now, you'll die. You have to fight to stay alive.* Somehow God provided me with sufficient strength to make the decision to go ahead with it.

The whole procedure took over two hours, and as my father and I left the building, it suddenly hit me that Bob and my mother were still out in the car. When I saw Bob, I wondered if she had told him.

"Let's talk when we get home," I said to him as we walked back to his car.

Bumper-to-bumper rush-hour traffic, the afternoon heat, and the exhaustion that was setting in made the trip home long and unpleasant. I couldn't believe that my morning and afternoon fit into the same day. For the first time, I was forced to place my growing love for Bob, and the joy that brought, side by side with the ugliness of the rape. I could no longer separate them into two worlds. Both were a part of my life, and somehow I had to learn to put them together.

My parents arrived home shortly before Bob and I did,

and Bob waited in the car while I went into the house. I found my mother in the kitchen.

"Bob and I are going over to the church to talk."

"You're going to tell him?" she asked.

"I have to. I have to explain what happened this afternoon, and I'm not going to lie to him. Don't hold supper for us."

"I doubt the church is open—"

I was already out the door.

Our church was only six blocks away. It was too short a ride to cram in all the praying I wanted to do on the way. *Oh, Lord, please give me the words to tell him. If he falls apart or gets angry, please give me the strength to handle that. If he no longer wants me, please help me to bear that. Oh, Lord, what will he say? How will he react? Please help me, Father.*

When we arrived at the church, the doors were locked. As we turned to try another entrance, I continued praying. *Dear Lord, now I'm asking You for a place to tell Bob. Please let it be my church. Please find a way.*

As we were walking away, the door behind us opened. The custodian was leaving for the day—and it had to be the grumpy one. Somehow we were able to convince this reluctant keeper of the house that we were trustworthy church members (even though Bob was not a member there) in need of a place to talk, and he let us in. I considered that a very definite, positive answer to my prayer, as I'd had problems in the past trying to use the church when there were not "adults" around.

As we entered the sanctuary, I was immediately comforted by its quiet beauty. The afternoon sun pouring through the stained-glass window at the front of the sanctuary radiated its colors throughout the huge room. The chancel was raised up a level of three steps, and it was on these steps that Bob and I seated ourselves. When I look back on it now, it seems so appropriate that we were there, so near to the cross, the symbol of both suffering and redemption.

"What did my parents tell you this morning . . . about what happened in the projects?" I began, my heart pounding.

"They just said that you had witnessed some sort of crime or something."

"Well, that's not exactly true. Did my mother tell you anything else when you were waiting in the car with her?"

"No. We listened to the Cubs game and talked about other stuff." I could tell by the look on his face that he sensed the seriousness of the situation.

"This isn't my day off, Bob. I've been home since Saturday night, and I don't think I'm going back."

"You're quitting your job?"

"I'm . . . not sure. I think so."

"Why?"

"I was more than just a witness to a crime . . . I was raped."

"Oh . . . Kay . . ." He put his arms around me and held me for a long time . . . in silence. I could feel his tears soaking into the shoulder of my blouse. Finally he spoke. "But I don't understand. I prayed so hard for you."

"I know." We held each other as if letting go would bring the world crashing in.

Then, Bob broke the embrace. He lifted my chin so that our eyes met.

"Kay, there's something I want you to know. . . . Nothing in the world can ever change my love for you."

5

My first court appearance was scheduled for Friday, July eleventh, the day after I had identified the rapist. I had done my homework, going over and over the details of the rape in my mind. *I have to get every last detail right or they won't believe me. If my story has changed even in the slightest, they'll think I'm lying. They'll believe him. Him! And not me. I've prepared my mind. But oh, God, how can I ever be ready for this? How could this have happened to me?* I couldn't believe it was me. It must be happening to someone else. It was like a bad TV show. If only I could just turn it off. Just turn it off and walk away.

I decided to wear a plain brown dress. It would show respect for the court to wear a dress, and this one was simple and modest. They couldn't think I asked for it or wanted it. They couldn't think that of me, could they? *They don't know me. They don't even know me!*

I stood beside the car staring up at the massive building across the street. *He* was somewhere inside that building. I quickly looked away. My mother stood waiting for my father as he dug in his pocket for parking meter money. What a trivial thing to have to worry about! We were trying to avoid a parking ticket, while in a few minutes I had to stand in front of a judge and tell him I was raped. And *he* would be right there!

Oh, God, why does he have to be there? What if I fall apart when I see him? What if I freeze? What if I can't even talk? What if he threatens me again? He could have a knife hidden in his sock! They always search prisoners, don't they? Don't they?

The lobby of the building was crowded with people. Prosecutors. Defense attorneys. Victims. Criminals. But who was who? I couldn't tell. What did I look like to them? In just a few minutes an entire courtroom of strangers would know . . . they would know that I had been raped.

The courtroom was on the fourth floor. My parents and I barely fit into an already packed elevator. The doors closed. I couldn't move. What if he was in there, too? What if the guy who raped me was in the same elevator? *I can't get out. I'm trapped! I can't even move. I have to look at everyone in this elevator. I can't see everyone. They're all staring at me. But I have to turn around to see. I have to see if he's in this elevator!*

I was the first one out when the heavy doors split their seams. I stood and watched as the crowd of people emptied through the opening. No, he had not been on the elevator. Thank God. But when would I have to see him? What if I just bumped into him in the hall?

This hall was buzzing with movement, too. People going every direction. Some carrying briefcases. Some wiping noses of noisy, impatient children. Some, like us, simply walking . . . not knowing what lay ahead for them that day.

The courtroom was hot and noisy. It wasn't at all like Perry Mason. A lady was changing a baby's diaper on one of the back benches. A baby? In a place like this? Coming toward me was a tall bleached-blonde wearing a black leather miniskirt and vest and white vinyl go-go boots. The room reeked of stale cigars. Flies buzzed in through the open windows. Instead of dress shirts, most of the men in the visitors' gallery were wearing dirty white T-shirts. One of them even had a pack of cigarettes rolled up in his sleeve!

We found a place about five rows from the front. My parents sat on either side of me, my father nearest the center aisle. Almost as soon as we were seated, a uniformed policeman sat down next to my father.

"Are you Mr. Marston?"

"Yes."

"I'm Officer Farrell."

My father had talked to him on the phone when he had called to tell us to be here today. He was also the arresting officer in my case.

"They have a few more cases before ours. Shouldn't be long, though."

A young kid dressed in blue jeans, a T-shirt, and a leather vest was brought in and placed directly in front of the judge.

"State your name." He did. "Your age."

"Fourteen."

"It says here that you assaulted Officer Thompson with a knife. Is that true?"

"Yes, sir."

"Have you ever been in trouble before?"

"No, sir."

With people all around us talking and rustling in their seats, it was difficult to hear the whole conversation. But I strained to hear as much as I could.

"I don't ever want to see you in my courtroom again. Do you understand?"

"Yes, sir."

"All right. Get out of here."

That was it. He was released. I watched the officer who had been assaulted as his face flushed with anger and frustration. Shaking his head in disgust, he turned and walked away.

I couldn't believe it! This kid had attacked a policeman with a knife, and he got a quick slap on the hand and was put back on the street. Is that what they would do to the guy who had raped me? A slap on the hand and back on the street?

Two more cases were heard and then . . .

"The State of Illinois vs. Roger Gray."

Officer Farrell stood up, looked at me, and said, "That's us."

So that was his name. Roger Gray. No one had told me what his name really was. As I moved out into the aisle, the side door opened and an officer led Roger Gray to the front. I placed myself as far from him as I could, with my father and two other men between us. As they spoke, I figured out that one was the defense attorney and the other was the district attorney who would be representing me. The district attorney spoke first.

"Your honor, we have not yet received the medical report from the crime lab, which is essential to our case. We wish to implore a continuance."

Turning to the defense attorney, the judge inquired, "Objection?"

"No, Your Honor."

"Two weeks. Hearing is set for 9:00 A.M., July 25."

The judge then addressed Roger Gray. "Since you don't have a record, bail is reduced to $5,000. Next case."

That was it? It was over? I was confused. What happened? As we turned to leave, Officer Farrell suggested to my father that we go to the coffee shop across the street from the courthouse to talk.

It was smoke filled and packed with people. By the time we found a table, I was bursting with questions.

"Was that man in the three-piece suit my lawyer?"

"Yes, that was the district attorney. He'll be presenting your case."

"Shouldn't I talk to him? He doesn't even know me."

"He couldn't possibly take time to talk to all the plaintiffs. He goes through a case every half hour in there. Besides, he has your statement and all the reports."

"So why didn't he say anything else? I thought I'd have to tell the whole story today."

"No, Kay. Do you remember those tests they took at the hospital?"

"What tests?"

"Well, they took one that should show the presence of sperm."

"Oh." Suddenly I became anxious, fidgeting with a napkin. Anyone could overhear our conversation.

"Those results haven't come back yet, so the district attorney asked for a continuance. That just means the hearing is delayed for two weeks or more."

"What do you mean, 'or more?' " my voice softened.

"Well, Roger Gray's attorney can ask for a continuance, too, if he wants to."

"Why would *he* want to?"

"Oh, just to have more time to prepare his defense. Sometimes it's a delay tactic. They figure if they can put it off, maybe you'll decide to drop the charges."

"How did he get that lawyer?" I asked.

"Beats me. His folks aren't even in town. They're on vacation. But he wasn't appointed by the court. That's his own lawyer."

"I didn't figure anyone in the projects could afford one. I don't understand why he gets to have his own lawyer and I don't."

"Well, see, rape is a crime against the state, so the state represents you. The district attorney will do fine. Don't worry."

"Well, at least he'll be in jail. [Later I learned that Roger Gray did raise the bail money and had spent only one night in jail.] Why did the judge reduce the bail? When I identified him, they told me he had a record."

"No. See, he's been arrested three times before. Once for grand theft, once for possession of narcotics, and I don't know what else. But they've never gotten a conviction on him. So the judge reduced it to $5,000. It had been set at $10,000. . . . Say, Kay, there is something you should think about. They'll probably try to get you to change your mind about the charge."

"About the charge? What do you mean?"

"Well, if you change it to assault rather than rape, they might have a better chance of convicting him."

"What do you mean? He didn't beat me up . . . he raped me! Why should I change it to assault?"

"Just think about it, Kay."

———

Officer Farrell had been right about two things. The district attorney did try to get me to reduce the charge to assault. I refused. And on July 25, Roger Gray's attorney did ask for a continuance. It was granted.

My third court appearance was on August 14, the preliminary hearing. The defense attorney asked for another continuance. He was definitely stalling. He must have known Deanna would not be available to testify in a couple of weeks.

"Your Honor," the district attorney spoke in my defense, "Deanna Harris, one of our key witnesses, is spending her junior year in college abroad. She leaves for France on September 9. The defense has had five weeks to prepare its case."

"We shall proceed with the hearing. Request for continuance denied."

I was directed to stand right next to Roger Gray, facing the judge. Mentally I put up a wall between us. Just because I had to stand next to him did not mean I had to look at him or even recognize that he was there. I would not.

The judge directed the first question to me.

"State your name, please."

My heart pounded. Part of my wall was coming down. Now he was going to find out who I was.

"Kay Marston," I mumbled.

"Speak up please, young lady."

"Kayleen Marston."

"How old are you?"

"Nineteen."

"It says you're a college student. What college do you attend?"

More of my wall crumbled . . . he'd know how to find me!

Before I could make myself say the words, my father, who had been standing behind me, interrupted. "Your Honor, Kayleen would rather not answer that question with *him* right here."

"You're the girl's father?"

"Yes."

The judge turned back to me. "You will answer the question, Kayleen."

I spoke softly. "Hope College."

The judge's response came loud and clear. "Hope College. Never heard of it. Where is it?"

What do you want from me? Why are you asking me *all the questions? Why don't you ask this Roger Gray something? He raped* me! *I didn't rape* him!

Bit by bit, question after question, my wall collapsed. I was stripped down . . . no protection, no defenses, naked in front of him once more. *Oh, God, he's doing it again. He's getting me again. Get me out of here. Oh, God, get me out!*

Officer Farrell told me afterward that the purpose of the hearing had been for the judge to decide whether or not there was sufficient evidence to proceed with the case. But I never understood why so much personal information had to be revealed. Maybe the judge had been testing me to see if I was serious about it and willing to go through with a trial. Whatever his reasons, he decided to send it on to the grand jury. The date was set for one week later.

6

By the time my parents and I walked up the endless steps inside the courthouse to the lobby, I was winded. Deanna and Rev were already there. They would be testifying in front of the grand jury today as well. As we walked toward them, I noticed a woman I had not seen before. Deanna turned to introduce her to us.

"Kay, Mr. and Mrs. Marston, this is my mother."

It wasn't until that moment that it occurred to me that this had been a rough experience for Deanna and Rev, too. I had been so wrapped up in getting myself through all of it that I had not considered the effect it would have on them. I began to appreciate what it had taken for them to even be there to support me in prosecuting Roger Gray. Deanna's mother lived 250 miles away, yet had come to be with her daughter for the grand jury hearing.

A voice interrupted my thoughts. "Come this way, please." We were led down a quiet, dimly lit hallway, closed off from the rest of the building, and were asked to wait on a wooden bench in the hall just outside the courtroom. Deanna was called in first.

My stomach was churning. I was wearing the same brown dress I had worn to court before. Fidgeting with one of the buttons, I began to let some of my nervousness out.

"I don't know if I can do this. What's taking them so long

in there, anyway?" *What am I doing here? Do I have to tell them everything? What if I can't answer their questions? I didn't know what climax was before. What if they ask me stuff like that again? Dear Lord, you got me through the rape. Please help me now.*

At that moment of confusion, frustration, nervousness, and fear, strength sufficient for the hour came through my mother's words.

"Kayleen, just do it for the other twenty-five girls he might rape if they don't get him off the street."

The thought grabbed my scattering fears. I might be saving somebody else from a rape by going through this now. It gave me a purpose, a reason to go on. I would cling to that thought throughout the questioning.

The massive courtroom door opened and Deanna came out. I was motioned to go in. As we passed each other, I whispered to her, "How'd it go?"

She managed a weak smile. "Okay, I guess."

As I entered the courtroom full of people, I saw only two familiar faces, the district attorney and the defense attorney. After being sworn in, I was directed to sit on a straight-backed chair in a boxed-in area, this time similar to the Perry Mason courtroom. The judge was sitting to my right, above and slightly behind me.

Directly in front of me was the jury. Fifteen men and women. They were seated behind three rows of raised senate-like desks, covering the whole width of the room. All eyes were focused on me.

The judge instructed me to relate my story. It had been well-rehearsed. Maybe too well-rehearsed. I told everything in detail, including conversation between Roger Gray and myself. The questions followed.

"Please clarify when it was that he kissed you on the street," a jury member asked.

"It was right after he raped—"

"Objection, Your Honor," the defense attorney cut in.

The judge spoke to the jury. "The jury will recognize 'alleged' rape."

"Will you please describe what was happening between

the time Miss Harris left and the time she returned with Reverend Quillan?" the same jury member asked.

"He was . . . raping me."

"Objection!" Roger Gray's attorney had jumped to his feet and yelled his objection, startling me.

This time the judge turned to me, "Young lady, you will refrain from using the word 'rape.' Rape has not been proven. You will answer the question please."

"He was . . . in me."

"Did you see him enter you?"

"I was staring at the ceiling. I didn't watch."

"I see. Then it could have been with his finger or anything else that he entered you?"

There was a pause. The judge spoke to me, "You will answer the question."

"No, it wasn't anything else . . . it was him."

"But you didn't see?"

"No." *Would that mean I wasn't raped?*

"How old are you?" another jury member asked.

"Nineteen."

"It says here that he's seventeen."

Two years younger than me. He was younger than me! I didn't have the chance to say in defense that he looked much older. Kids in the city had mistaken me for fourteen. The hardness of the city had not had time to touch my face the way it had the young people who had grown up there . . . the way it had toughened him. All they heard was that I was nineteen and he was seventeen, two years my junior.

"How tall are you?"

"Five-feet-seven." I knew what they were thinking. He was only slightly taller.

"How much do you weigh?"

"125."

"It says here that he weighs less than that."

Why were they asking all this? They had all this information in front of them. What were they trying to prove? That I should have been able to overpower him? What about his buddies out in the street who were waiting for us? What about all the threats? All they wanted to know was who was bigger? What about the knife in his back pocket?

"Did you see his knife? Did he pull it on you?"

"No, but he kept reaching for it saying, 'I don't want to hurt you.' Over and over he said that."

"Did you see it?"

I couldn't believe it. Everyone knew that absolutely all the teenage guys and girls in the projects carried knives, often switchblades. I had no reason to doubt that he had one in his pocket. Should it have occurred to me in that moment of terror for my life that this attacker might be younger, might weigh less, and might possibly be bluffing about a knife in his pocket?

"Did you actually see the weapon?"

"No!"

But it was there. . . . They didn't know! How could they know?

"Why didn't you ring the doorbells on the mailboxes?"

"I, uh, don't . . . know . . . I . . . guess I didn't think of it."

"Why didn't you scream?"

"I don't know."

The district attorney was given the floor. He asked only one question.

"Kayleen, did you know Roger Gray before the day in question?"

"No, I had never seen him before."

The defense attorney asked only one question as well.

"Is it possible that Roger Gray could have known you?"

"I don't think—"

"Is it possible?"

"Well, I suppose he might have seen me—"

"That's all, Your Honor."

The judge turned to me. "Thank you. You may step down."

I was confused. Something wasn't right. When I was back in the hallway, a thought surfaced.

"Rev," I asked, "are there doorbells on the mailboxes in those apartment buildings?"

"No, why?"

"They tricked me! Oh, no! They asked why I didn't ring

the doorbells on the mailboxes! Rev, you've gotta tell them there aren't any. When you go in there, could you tell them that? Please?"

"I'll do what I can, Kay."

Rev was called in next. As I sat there on the bench waiting for him to come out, my anger grew like a fire in a dry field. After ten or fifteen minutes, he walked out looking pale.

"Did you tell them, Rev—about the doorbells?"

"No, Kay, I didn't get a chance."

The district attorney soon joined us.

"Well, all we do is wait now," he said.

"What about Roger Gray? Doesn't he have to be here?" I asked.

"They heard his side of the case yesterday. They should have a decision before too long."

"You mean today? Right now?"

"Most likely. I'll be back as soon as I know something. It would probably be best if you all wait right here." With that, he went back down the long hall, the same way he had come.

Not more than fifteen or twenty minutes later, he returned.

"Mr. and Mrs. Marston and Kayleen, will you come with me, please?" Rev and Deanna and her mother were left on the bench in the hall, while he led us to a small conference room. Once there, he looked directly at me as he spoke.

"The jury reached their decision. They didn't indict him."

"There won't be a trial?"

"No."

"It's over?"

"Yes."

He won't go to jail, I thought. Relief. Tremendous relief. The minimum sentence would have been twenty years, they had told me. Now I didn't have to worry that he might blame me for sending him to prison and come after me when he got out. . . . But—wait a minute. They believed him? Not me!

"They didn't believe me!"

"It's not a question of whether they believed you or not. They might very well have believed your story."

"What do you mean? You said they didn't indict him."

"Actually, they're doing you a favor by not going to trial with this case. They're saving you the trouble of going through all that. Their decision just means they don't think there is sufficient evidence for a conviction."

"What do you mean? I had two witnesses!"

"Neither one saw the act itself. It was your word against—"

"But the hospital lab report proved penetration."

"Yes, but they couldn't prove it wasn't willing on your part. It's tough to convict on these cases. They don't usually get 'em unless they can hang up torn and bloody clothes for evidence. Usually then it goes to homicide anyway."

They couldn't prove it wasn't willing on your part . . . they couldn't prove it wasn't willing on your part . . . they couldn't prove it wasn't willing. . . . The words echoed through my head. What did I have to do? Show them scars and broken bones? All I wanted was to stay alive. Willing on my part? *Oh, God. What do they think I am? What do they think I am?*

———

One of the questions asked by the grand jury that day remained unanswered for a long time, even in my own mind: Why didn't I scream? The answer was more complicated than any of the jury members could have imagined, and in order to answer it, I had to go back in my mind to that late afternoon in the projects. . . .

Deanna and I were more afraid of street brawls and gang fights than anything else. We knew that being out on those streets on a Saturday night after dark was quite dangerous. Besides, I had been brought up not to be out in any unsure situation after dark. It was that "after dark on the city streets" phenomenon that made Deanna and me decide to split up. We had a lot of leaflets to deliver. If we stayed together, we would not get home before the streets were unsafe. So we split up.

Even though it was the first time I had been alone on the inner-city streets, I felt relatively sure of myself. I was in my own neighborhood—not more than two blocks from Rev's house and our apartment. Deanna was on one side of the street and I was on the other. We could even see each other from time to time as we went from building to building. And the street was crawling with kids. Somehow there was a feeling of safety where children were playing.

With all the people on the street and Deanna close by, it didn't occur to me that I could be in danger . . . that I could be snatched at any moment and raped or killed in an entryway to an apartment building. Besides, I was doing God's work. Nothing could happen to me. Not me. Not there. Not then. Not ever. God would take care of me.

I think it was this disbelief, this failure to recognize that anything so terrible could happen to me, that kept me, in part, from screaming. In the first few moments when I was confronted by Roger Gray, I did not allow myself to believe I was in danger. The moment he grabbed my breasts, I knew I was in real trouble, but by that time I was past the point of a reactionary scream—by that I mean the kind of scream you let loose when somebody jumps out at you from behind a bush.

When reality did hit, it hit hard. My assailant had a knife. I was in his world, not mine. He had been drinking. *His* friends were waiting for him out on the street. *His* friends would come if I screamed. Or would anyone come? This was not my world. In my world if anything looked suspicious, someone would call the police, who would be there within a few minutes. This was not suburbia. This was the inner city of Chicago. Here they shouted, "Pigs!" at policemen driving by in their cruisers. Who would get involved? And even if someone did, how long would it take the police to come on a Saturday night? Sometimes it took a half hour or more for them to answer a call. I could hear voices outside, but it did not mean help for me. Who would get involved—to help me?

Besides, if I screamed he might kill me. I couldn't get past him to get out the door. I couldn't talk him out of it.

He didn't care if I had VD or my period. Fainting had not helped. He just dragged me down the stairs. If I screamed, he would shut me up. . . . *Please don't hurt me any more. I won't scream. Please don't kill me. I won't scream. Please. . . .*

Subconsciously, I was aware of all these elements at the time I was raped; yet when the jury member asked why I didn't scream, I had no answer. I had not been able to work through all of this. I just didn't know.

But none of this would matter. Finding the answers after the hearing couldn't change the outcome. It was over.

A trial could have meant trips home from college for court appearances; it might have dragged on for a year or more. So I was set free as well. I would never have to see *him* again! *Oh, God, it's over. It's really all over!*

7

My days at home following the court proceedings passed quickly. Since the jewelry store where I had worked the previous summer was in need of part-time help, I was able to get a job clerking four days a week. Much of my free time was spent seeing friends from high school days, visiting Bob, and preparing for the return to college in the fall.

Though I managed to keep myself busy, this period of time at home did not pass without incident. We all tried to leave the rape behind, never talking about it except when necessary.

Since my sister was only thirteen, my parents chose not to tell her what had happened to me. She didn't know about it until several years later when I told her myself. My older brother, Mark, knew soon after it happened. He and I were always close, and I wished I could spend more time with him. But his summer job at the railroad kept him away from home much of the time.

Both my parents and I wanted to shove the whole experience in the closet and close the door on it. Unfortunately, we could not. I didn't realize it at the time, but throughout the hearings I had been denying many of my own feelings about the rape itself in order to emotionally endure the ordeal. I had convinced myself I was strong and in control when actually I had not faced the multitude of negative feelings that were yet to surface.

A perfect example of this denial is revealed in a portion of a letter I wrote to Bob just after the grand jury's decision.

> There's nothing to worry about anymore. It's all over. Bob, I have never felt so grateful to be alive. I could have been killed. But God didn't let that happen. It feels so good just to be alive. Everything's going to be OK now.

My parents had denied many of their emotions as well, but this could not last. The night that my father's repressed anger over the rape was initially unleashed was a terrible night for all of us.

It was a Saturday night. I had gone to the basement to iron a blouse I needed for church the next day. It was early evening, and the heat of the day had not yet lifted its hold upon us. I stood over the ironing board, beads of sweat rolling down my temple past my ear. There was tension in the air—the kind that comes when humidity and heat drain from us such virtues as patience and even tolerance for one another. I felt as one does between the time the lightning flashes and the thunder claps in a violent storm. An uneasiness . . . a restlessness.

When the hard, fast footsteps stormed down the stairs, I knew I was the target of their approach. It was my father's feet that first spoke of his irrepressible anger as they deliberately shook each step of the stairs on the way down. A shudder crept down my spine.

My father's yelling was something I had learned to tolerate but could never get used to. As his rage tore through me, my body responded . . . my stomach beginning to churn, my arms and face becoming hot, my legs begging to be relieved of my body's weight. But I would take this standing up.

"What were you doing out there at night? You should have known better! If you hadn't been out there, it never would have happened!"

"I was doing my job! It was my job to be there!"

I couldn't believe it. He was blaming me. It was not my

fault! I never asked Roger Gray to rape me! *I am not a slut. You can't blame me. I won't let you!*

Never in my life had I ever yelled back at my father. Even now I couldn't scream at him, except in my mind. But I could do the next best thing, and I did. I walked out on him in the midst of his explosion of anger. I yanked the cord of the iron from the socket. Without a single word, I glared hate at him, then briskly and feverishly escaped by way of the basement door.

I would never go back there. He was not my father. He was hateful . . . mean . . . cruel. I would never see him or speak to him again. As the door slammed behind me, I could still hear yelling.

"Where do you think you're going?"

"Well, she needs somebody," my brother accused.

"Don't you press her for any details."

I was half a block away when Mark caught up with me. We walked together in silence. All my energy was being consumed by my muscles, held tight in tension. Gradually my speech took over the job of letting the anger out.

"I'm never going back there, ever."

"He's just angry. He'll cool off."

"Just angry? He blamed me for it. He thinks it's all *my* fault!"

"Give him some time. He doesn't know how to deal with all this."

"Why should *I* have to be the one to give to *him*? What about me? Doesn't he care at all about me?"

"I think he feels really guilty, Kayleen."

"Guilty? For what?"

"For letting you go there."

"That's stupid. That was my decision. It was my job. I should be back there right now. I don't know how Deanna's doing it all herself."

"He could have insisted that you not go in the first place. He must wish he had now. I just think he couldn't face blaming himself, so he blew up at you."

"Great. That's just great. So why doesn't Mother say anything? She never talks about it."

"I don't know, Kayleen. I just don't know."

We walked for what seemed like three or four miles. It was past the time when you could hear mothers calling from their front doors, "Didn't you see the streetlight go on? Time to come in."

Somehow as Mark and I talked, I was able to calm down enough so that my anger turned to hurt and terrible disappointment. Not only did I have to face the fact of being raped, but now my own father was blaming me for it—blaming me for all the shame, the humiliation, the pain, the terror, all the awful things I was feeling. They were not caused by something I had done. They were caused by what Roger Gray had done to me. Yet my father was blaming me and my mother couldn't talk about it. I couldn't handle it all. It would be easier to simply reject my parents.

But I couldn't face a separation from them at this point in my life, either. If I walked out on my family now, I would have no one else to turn to . . . nowhere to go. I was too terrified to go back to the city. Besides, I was still a part of my father's household. I couldn't bear to lose my home on top of everything else.

When we got back to the house, I took a deep breath and slowly climbed the seven cement steps leading to the front door. The squeak of the screen door announced my arrival. My father did not look up as I walked over to the chair where he was sitting. It had been a long time since I had kissed my father. Physical affection was not often shown between us. It took every muscle in my body to lean over and place a kiss on his cheek. He sat firmly planted in his chair and did not speak. Nor did I.

I went directly to my room. There I began to sort out all the feelings that had surfaced. When I kissed my father, I had felt a kind of power rise within me. In spite of all he had done to me, I was able to come back . . . to forgive him with a kiss. My kiss must have humiliated him, made him feel sorry for what he had said. Was that forgiveness? Or was it retaliation? Deep inside, I think I wanted it to be both.

I had not been the only victim of Roger Gray's rape.

Everyone close to me had been damaged as well. Each had his or her own feelings and emotions to deal with, not unlike my own. Unfortunately, at that time I desperately needed their support.

Being a parent myself now, I can look back with a certain appreciation for what my parents must have been going through. They had their own shock, disgust, and guilt to handle as well as having to deal with me. But at the time I was bitterly angry and emotionally devastated by my father's outburst. It hurt for a long time. I could more easily reject him than accept his limitations. He was not a person who could cry his feelings out in tears. Nor was it easy for him to talk about them. When his feelings were finally released in anger, I was their target, since I was the one who had brought the crisis home.

Not until several years later was I able to fully forgive my father for blaming me for the rape. Before I could take that step, however, I had to acknowledge that he would not, could not, always live up to my expectations.

It wasn't the first time I had come to this realization about my father. At the tender age of seven I had been forced to see that he was not a god . . . that he was human. I think that realization hurt more than anything else—more than skinned knees, more than my brother's punches in the arm. Until that time, my father had been infallible. The realization came through an experience my brother Mark and I shared one summer. . . .

One day Mark and I, at a loss for things to do, managed to get into a "my dad's bigger than your dad" conversation with Jimmy, one of the neighbor kids. He and my brother were in the second grade together. When Jimmy bragged that his dad ate chocolate-covered ants and frog legs, Mark was not to be outdone. Spotting a yellow jacket buzzing by, he replied, "Well, my dad eats bee sandwiches."

"He does not."

"He does so."

"Does not."

"Does so. Go ask him."

I was so intent on proving my brother right and my father the hero Mark was making him out to be that I actually allowed myself to believe it was true. Our small, but brand-new house had a huge, treeless backyard, and the grass was filled with clover that attracted all kinds of bees. Maybe my father did eat bee sandwiches. I chimed into the bickering, sticking up for my brother all the way into the house.

We found my dad, who promptly said that sure, he loved bee sandwiches, but that he wouldn't eat one unless it had *fifty* bees in it. He probably thought that would put an end to the matter. Obviously my father had not spent as much time in the backyard as we had. We knew we could find fifty bees if we really tried. On our way out, we stopped at the kitchen junk drawer and picked out three of the biggest, fattest rubber bands you ever saw.

"What are we going to do with these?" I asked, like a tagalong little sister.

"We're going bee hunting, stupid," Mark said.

Well, I wasn't too keen on that idea because I had been stung by a bee the summer before. It had made my whole face swell up, and I was so sick from it that I had to stay in for a whole day. But my loyalty to my brother and my pride in my father won out over my fears. So I took one of the makeshift slingshots and marched out right alongside my big brother on the big bee hunt.

By suppertime, we had collected forty-three bees, but my dad insisted that it wasn't a bee sandwich until we had fifty. We had a difficult time finding the last seven bees, but later that same evening we managed to present my dad with fifty yellow jackets and wasps. After they had been stunned by the slap of the rubber band, Mark had picked them up with a straight pin and stuck them to the bottom of an overturned cardboard box. When we handed the box to my dad, some of them were still squirming under their pins.

My father insisted that though he loved bees, he just didn't have the heart to eat any that were still moving. He suggested that we put them in the freezer and he would eat them the next day. I don't know how we could have agreed to that. The suspense was killing us. But we said we would wait until the next day.

Jimmy was knocking at our door early the next morning. The three of us stood around my dad with our big, round eyes bugging out of their sockets. First he spread butter on two slices of bread, then carefully placed each of the fifty bees on the buttered bread. As he put the top slice on the sandwich, he said, "You know, I'm really not hungry enough to eat it now. I'll eat it later." Three small sighs came out of three small bodies like air rushing out of a balloon.

"I'll just put it back in the freezer like this and have it later."

Sometime later that afternoon on one of our many trips back to the freezer to check on the sandwich, we found that it was gone. We ran to find my dad, who said, "Yes, bee sandwiches sure are delicious."

Proud in his victory, Mark turned to Jimmy and uttered the inevitable, "See, I told you so." It was like Peter Pan. We all believed.

Two days later was garbage pickup day. The garbage cans had been taken out to the street as usual. It was there that Mark and I would sometimes scrounge through the trash to see if any of our junky but prized possessions had been thrown out. We were carefully thumbing through it when—we both gasped simultaneously in shock and disappointment. There, halfway down the can, partially stuck to the side, was the bee sandwich. He had not eaten it after all.

Needless to say, we never told Jimmy.

Recalling this incident several years later, I remembered those first feelings of disillusionment. By then I was old enough to understand that my father was human, and that although he might sometimes hurt or disappoint me, he was still my father and he still loved me.

Lord, please help me to stop expecting my father to be more than he is.

8

It was dark. Someone was chasing me. No. He wasn't running. Neither was I, but I was so out of breath! He was following me. I couldn't tell who it was . . . just a dark figure, a flowing, nondescript form. I tried to scream, but I couldn't make a sound. "I'm going to get you!" Closer . . . closer . . . suddenly I saw his face. At that same instant I saw the pistol. He grabbed me by the neck and I stopped breathing. The gun was pressed into my temple so hard that it hurt. It went off three times. I heard it blast right through my head.

I sat straight up in bed screaming. I always thought when you had nightmares you were supposed to wake up before you died. I guess I woke up in the split second between the time the gun went off and the time I was to die. I was sweating and hysterical. I knew the face in my dream. It was my father. That made it even more horrible.

My mother and father both heard me scream and came running into my room. I only wanted my mother's comfort. I was exhausted, but too terrified to go back to sleep. I had never had a nightmare before. Unlike most of my dreams, I could remember every detail of it . . . every feeling . . . every sound . . . but I couldn't repeat any of it to my mother. It was too horrid.

The same nightmare recurred several times during the

71

few months that followed. Not until the third or fourth time did I discover that a pattern had been established: the terrible nightmares always occurred on the fifth day of my menstrual cycle, and I had been raped on the fifth day of my cycle. Each succeeding dream was less terrifying than the previous one, and almost as soon as I discovered the pattern, the dreams ceased.

Until the nightmares, I had convinced myself I was through with the rape. Even after my father's emotional outburst, I had tried to go on with my life as if the rape had never happened. Since the court proceedings were over, I figured I should be finished with it all. I had set up a type of bargain. By not talking about it, I would not have to experience the pain: my own pain, Bob's pain, my parents' pain. Another result of the bargain was that because I wasn't talking about it, they weren't either. We all played the game of pretending that it never happened. For a while it worked, but eventually my denial gave way to depression.

The first indication that something was still wrong came with the first nightmare. Shortly after that Bob and I returned to college. We saw each other every day, and almost that often I was given assurances that his love for me had not changed. Yet I knew something was wrong. The following is from a letter I sent across campus to him soon after we returned to school in September.

> I'm getting so used to hearing you tell me that you love me that I feel like it's just the convenient thing to say. I know you mean it when you say it, but . . .

I knew it in my head, but I was beginning to have trouble *feeling* his love for me in my heart. I went on in the letter to ask him if he would call me more often or send me notes. I had begun to feel less and less special to Bob. I needed to have him tell me constantly and in many different ways that he still cared about me. These feelings were a result of my beginning to face up to my pain. I had been violated. A stranger off the street had held the power to steal away my dignity, my significance. I was beginning to *feel* that, and it showed up in my relationship with Bob. In a note to him, I wrote:

I don't want you to feel like you have to spend money on me . . . one dandelion that would remain in a vase until it was totally wilted and then would go in a scrapbook to remind me in future days that, one day in the past, Bob made an ordinary day special by going out of his way to make a girl feel like a princess again. I guess I just want to feel like that special person to you that you tell me I am.

From deep inside the feelings of dirtiness and ugliness and worthlessness had finally begun to surface. As a result, I desperately wanted to feel like a beautiful princess deserving all the attention of a court of attendants.

Bob did try to make me feel special. I'll never forget the time he and a friend came to my dorm and surprised me with a huge arrangement of flowers. They had been out in the country on his friend's motorcycle and had come across an elderly woman selling flowers from her garden. Bob rode all the way back on the cycle holding a five-pound coffee can full to overflowing with the homegrown flowers. It was the most beautiful assortment I had ever seen, and I will always remember how very special it made me feel.

But in spite of all Bob's attention, I was unable to keep the mountain of negative emotions from overshadowing whatever brief moments of joy I had. I fell deeper and deeper into depression, becoming two different emotional beings. I was either extremely high or extremely low, unable to find a medium level of stability.

My highs were unhealthy bursts of energy. At times I was ridiculously silly and turned into the hall clown in our dorm. I was the source of many a laugh as I would sneak into a friend's room to sew her pant legs together, put cornflakes in her bed, glue her shoes to the floor, or blitz the entire room with toilet paper. Everyone around me was having a good time, and although I was the source of their fun, inside I ached. The laughing hurt, and I was alone.

My lows were dangerously low. I would become so depressed that I was almost in a trance. Often I would sit in the cold, open stairway of the dorm with my guitar and sing sad songs, wallowing in the emptiness of the echo that came from my hollow surroundings. If the songs weren't sad enough, I would write songs that were. If I was not singing, I was quiet and alone with my thoughts. I did not think about the rape during these times. Instead, I fantasized more pain—imagining Bob leaving me or someone I loved being killed. My grades began to reflect these lows as I cut classes to sit alone in a cold corner or walk the campus in silence.

My dates with Bob were often a combination of these highs and lows. He could never predict when his seemingly carefree, fun-loving date would suddenly lapse into a state of depression. I can only imagine how helpless he must have felt as he watched my moods fluctuate during those times. I was riding an emotional roller coaster; while at the top I found escape from the pain at the bottom. As time passed, the gap between my highs and lows would narrow. But before that happened, I hit rock bottom.

> O God, my God, why have you gone from me,
> Far from my prayers, far from my cry?
> To you I call, and you never answer me;
> You send no comfort, and I don't know why.
> Into your hands I commend my spirit, O Lord;
> Into your hands I commend my heart,
> For I must die to myself in loving you;
> Into your hands I commend my love.[1]

I was praying this song as I sat on the inside back stairway of the three-story brick dorm and sang with my guitar . . . calling out to my God, the God who had called me to serve Him in the city—that awful, dirty, horrible city that had swallowed me and spit me back out again to walk the earth a beaten creature. The steps were hard and cold, as hard and cold as the depths I was reaching as I poured out these words with voice and tears.

> You've been my guide since I was very young;
> You showed the way when I needed someone's hand.

---

[1] "Into Your Hands" by Ray Repp (refrain adapted to first-person singular), K&R Music, Inc., Trumansburg, N.Y. (Used by permission.).

And now I'm lonely; nobody's by my side;
Stay near, my Lord, and be my friend.[2]

Despite my despair, I was very aware of God's presence as I sang. He was the only one who really knew what I was feeling. He could see the aching hole inside me—the emptiness that no one else could see. Even though I couldn't believe that void would ever go away, it was a comfort to know that He knew my pain.

But, God, how can You be the same God to whom I committed my life, the same God who loved and cared for me in the past? I know You're there, God, but how could You leave me so alone? I sang, searching for answers I could not find. Was there no one who could take that emptiness from me? Often I would start out singing in anger, "O God, my God, why have you gone from me? You send no comfort, and I don't know why." I would sing it over and over and over again until my anger dissolved into a tranquil sadness.

I was singing to God, but I did not feel close to Him. He was somewhere way off in the distance, hearing me, watching me, but, for some cruel reason unknown to me, choosing not to come close to me—not to give me answers. I was alone and would always be . . . alone.

O Lord,
How can I give of myself when I can no longer believe
   in myself?
How can I love when I cannot give of myself?
How can I trust when You send no comfort in the
   blackest night?
You say that You open doors, yet I cannot find these
   doors.
I am caught in a giant web. I cannot see my foe.
What is it that has caught me in its web?
Is it circumstance or tragic fate?
Is it You, God?
Or another person?
Who has done me wrong?
And, oh, Lord, how do I get out?

---

[2]Ibid.

My arms are outstretched. I cry aloud.
Yet, no one hears.
The deadening silence is driven into my head,
    and back out again.
Thundering, throbbing.
Why? Why?
Where is the answer?
O Lord, shine a light, for I need it.
Give me hope and strength.
For I am weak and ready to fall.
Don't let me fall, O Lord.
Don't let me fall.

9

In October, I wrote the following letter to God:

Why, Lord, why?

I can't take this life. It's too much for me. I have asked you many times for help, but I can't ever find it. I'm weak, Lord. I'm not who I was. I used to be so happy with life—it used to excite me when I would see someone else smile. Now I don't care, no one is smiling anymore. Nothing is beautiful. All is ugly. I try, Lord. I try to forget, but it haunts me. I can't forget it and I can't accept it. It haunts me. It is tearing me apart. I need help. I ask for it, but no one speaks—everything is silent. I can't stand the silence. It's driving me crazy. All communication is lost. People are not people. They are inhabitants of this same lonely world that I walk in but can't live in. Oh, God, where is your strength?

I want to leave this life—I want to die. A bottle of aspirin—a knife in the chest—oh, God, it would be so easy for me to do it now. Whence cometh my help?

I want to be myself again. I want so much to be happy and make others happy. But I need help and I'm not finding it.

Every face is a brick wall that says "be happy," huh—"be happy—be happy—what's wrong? What's wrong?" For God's sake everyone knows what's wrong. Why can't somebody help me?

Let's talk about it—oh, God, what good can it do? Who can help—can anyone?

I loved a man and he loved me—but how can he love a nothing anymore? He is losing out. I am pulling him down. Lord, my whole personage has changed. What's the matter?— What's the matter? The word is despair. Lord, I'm giving up— but you can't give up—but you can't go on—but you can't give up—but you can't go on.

How can I be a witness for Christ when I can't feel His strength when I need it?

And oh, God, why won't you ever let me cry when I need to?

If I really loved Bob I would leave him because I am making his life ugly with my sorrows. I am burdening him with my grief and it hurts me to see him burdened. Yet I keep doing it. Oh, God, how bad?

I want to run away—but I can't go home—everything stares me straight in the face there. It's worse there. I can't go anywhere, Lord. . . . it's something I can't shake. It follows me everywhere. There's no out. Oh, God, get me out. Get me out. I can't take it anymore.

Where is all the love you promised me?

I am looking at a plastic world. I try to smile at the people but their faces are plastered stuck. There is no response to my plea for help. Everything is a brick wall. A brick wall—a brick wall and my head hurts from beating against it—my head hurts—everything hurts—it hurts, oh help.

———

When I first read my suicide letter to God, ten years after I had written it, I was most appalled by the fact that I had even considered killing myself with a knife. It was a solemn reminder of how deeply I had hurt; an actual blade in the chest could not have equaled the intensity of the pain I had been experiencing. Seeing the letter in my own handwriting made it all too real. This person, so alone and so forsaken that she wanted to die, was me. Me!

During my deepest depression over the rape, I talked with many people. In addition to Bob, my roommate, and other friends in the dorm, I also spoke once or twice with my college chaplain. They all listened and tried to reach out to me, but I still felt alone in the world. Although I needed them to care for me, more than anything else I needed them to understand my anguish, my pain. But no one could.

Often during that time I wished I could talk to another rape victim, just to know that someone else in the world knew how horrible rape could be. In recent years I have talked with many victims of rape. Strongly believing that each person's pain is as individual as that person, I will never say, "I know how you feel." Yet it does help to talk with someone who has experienced the same level of pain— such as one rape victim with another, or one widow with another, or one paraplegic with another. And fortunately today there are countless sexual assault centers where trained listeners offer valuable information and support.

But back then I knew of no one who could share, either from special training or from personal experience, what I would call my level of suffering. Because I felt so alone, I felt separated . . . no longer a part of the world around me.

The horrible night that follows is vivid in my memory. It occurred within days of the writing of the suicide letter. . . .

———

Three o'clock in the morning and I was still awake. Jan, my roommate, had been sleeping for several hours. I was alert and very aware of one particular object in the dark room in which I lay . . . a large bottle of aspirin. It wasn't even mine. Jan had been downtown that day and had brought back several items from the drugstore, one of which was a bottle of those little white pain-killing tablets. That's what I needed. Something to stop the hurt.

As I lay there with my eyes wide open in the quiet darkness, the bottle became more and more obvious to me, as if it were the only object in a totally evacuated room. I could almost hear it call to me. . . . "Come and get me. I will kill your pain."

For several days I had thought about how I might kill myself. This way, if I took the pills and just got quietly back into bed, no one would know what I had done until morning. By then it would all be over. My only concern was that Jan would be the one to find me. How traumatic that would be for her. But it would have to be this way. Any other way would be so gruesome.

I slipped out of bed quietly, so I wouldn't disturb Jan, and carefully picked up the bottle of aspirin and a glass. The dimly lit hallway was deserted. As I pushed open the door to the bathroom, I was nearly blinded by the bright lights inside. I sat down on the cold tile floor with my back against the wall and stared at the bottle in my hand.

Oh, God, I am sinking. The weight is carrying me down. I can't hold myself up any longer. It's too much, Lord . . . too much. Oh, God, why?

Why? How could You let this happen to me when I gave up my summer to serve You? What about all the slutty, sinful people on this earth? It should have been them, not me. I never deserved that. My standards for living have always been high. I have not only been good, I have served You, God. How could You let this happen to me? Why, God? Why me?

The tone of my supplication was not angry, but low and desperate. I felt forsaken and unloved. And if God himself had forsaken me, who on earth would care for me? Still, the "Why?" surfaced above all the other questions.

I can't explain why I never opened that bottle. Even though I hated God, He still was God, and I never doubted His existence. I only wondered what kind of a monster He could be. He had been real to me in the past. He was real to me at that moment, though I despised Him for the cruelty He displayed by allowing me to suffer so.

I guess at that time I believed that if I killed myself, I would go straight to hell, that there would be no time for forgiveness. But that in itself did not scare me. I couldn't imagine that hell could be worse than what I was living then. What bothered me was that I would never know *why* God had let it happen. Why? That one-word question haunted me enough to leave a reason for living just a little longer.

I went back to bed as the sun was rising.

10

I did not tell anyone about the night I nearly took my own life until several weeks later, not even Bob. Somehow, I was able to find ways to make each day lead to the next, and the weeks passed. My periods of lowest depression over the rape became less and less frequent, and gradually I was able to resume normal activities. Though I still occasionally cut classes, I was able to handle almost a full schedule again by mid-November. I spent less time alone and more time with my friends and with Bob.

All along, Bob had tried very hard to keep me going. He had shared in many of my lowest moments and had been the vehicle of strength and hope through which God had come to me time after time. But I didn't see God at work then. I only saw Bob. He became my knight in shining armor, my white knight, as I called him. I adored him.

More than anything else, Bob and I enjoyed taking long walks together. Often on a Friday night we would walk downtown or to the park near the college. On one particularly chilly November night, we decided to brave the cold and walk to the track where Bob had run many meets the spring before. We sat down on the hard bleachers, staring at the deserted field in silence. A pleasant silence. We were together, really together.

"Bob, do you ever wonder what it will be like five or ten years from now?"

"What do you mean?"

"Oh, I mean do you think we'll be together then?"

"Oh, probably. We'll probably be married and have sixteen kids."

"Good grief! I hope not. Two or three would be plenty. . . . Do you ever think about that, Bob?"

"About what?"

"About being married and having kids?"

"Oh, I suppose, once in a while."

"You do?"

"Sometimes, I guess, but mostly I just think about you."

"About me? What do you think about when you think about me?"

"Oh, mostly about loving you."

I responded with an impish smile, jumped up, and bounded to the top of the bleachers. "Would you follow me anywhere?" I yelled down to him.

"What are you doing?"

"Do you love me?" I yelled, choking back a giggle.

"Of course I love you, you flake."

"Then would you follow me anywhere?"

"That's a dumb question. What are you doing up there?"

"I'm waiting for you to come love me up here."

"You're crazy!" With that he leaped up and chased after me.

As he ran up diagonally in one direction, I fled down the other way. I reached the ground first and tore off around the track. Bob was not far behind when he stopped and called out to me.

"I'll give you a quarter of a lap head start, and I'll still catch up with you."

"No, you won't! You'll have to hop a plane to catch me."

I had run about three-quarters of the way around the track when I could feel his feet pounding the asphalt behind me. I turned my head just briefly to see where he was and then kicked out a burst of speed. But Bob had a kick left, too. I should have known that from watching him run races on this track. I felt his hand on my neck and immediately surrendered, slowing down to a walk.

"I won!" I hollered, puffing and panting.

"You did not!" Bob laughed, not in the least winded.

"I did so . . . I got you, didn't I?"

I fell to the ground, lying on my back with my arms and legs outstretched. I stared up into the sky, laughter dancing in my eyes.

Bob stood directly above me, no longer laughing. He looked down at me intently. "You're so beautiful, Kayleen."

I knew how to respond when he called me Kayleen. I knew what he was thinking, what he was feeling. I felt it, too. He leaned down and tenderly kissed my cheek, my neck, my lips.

"Let's go," he said softly.

"Where?"

"How about Graves Hall?"

Bob and I had been there together before. In the basement of the stately old classroom building were music practice rooms where we knew we could find privacy.

He stood up, extending both hands toward me. I placed my hands in his. As he gently pulled me up, he put his arms around me and our lips met again. *If only the walk back to campus wasn't so long,* I thought to myself.

. . . As we descended the basement steps of the massive stone building, I was glad we hadn't seen anyone. I didn't want to share my world with anyone but Bob that night, not even to say hi. Even though none of the practice rooms were occupied, we chose the one at the end of the hall where no one would bother us. There, in the tiny secluded room, behind a mammoth old electric organ, Bob and I embraced. As we held each other in that still moment, our passion radiated through us.

Bob had not touched me since the rape. His touch felt wonderful. His touch felt wretched. I was torn. My feelings . . . a mass of confusion.

"Bob—"

"Oh, Kay, you feel so good."

"Oh, Bob, I . . . love being here with you." *No, I don't. I don't think I even like it. Why do I feel so dirty?* "We better go, Bob. What if somebody finds us here?"

"Don't be silly. There's no one around."

"But . . . we better go . . . it's . . . getting late."

"Kay, what's wrong?"

"I don't know. I just want to go. Will you walk me back?"

"But Kay—"

"Please, Bob, please walk me back now."

It was only a block to my dorm. A short, quiet walk. I went straight to my room, grabbed my john pail and a towel, and headed for the bathroom. Why did I feel like this? Ashamed. We hadn't done anything wrong. We weren't going to do anything wrong. We were just enjoying each other. So why did I feel so filthy? I took the shower at the end of the row. No one was near the showers. So why did I feel so self-conscious about undressing?

As I stepped into the shower, I became very aware of my breasts. *Don't look at them. They're ugly. I wish they weren't a part of me at all. Oh, God, what's wrong with me?* I put soap all over me. But it wasn't enough. More soap. *I can't get clean. How ugly! How dirty!* I stood in the shower for what must have been twenty minutes trying desperately to get clean. *I must get rid of those dirty hands yanking off my bra, feeling all over me. Dirty, dirty hands. Get your hands off me. They're my breasts. This is my body. You can't have it. Nobody can. Leave me alone. Don't touch me. Don't touch me. I can't stand to be touched. Dirty hands. Dirty hands. Let me up. Get off me. I will never be clean. Dirty, dirty hands. I can't get those awful hands off me. Get them off. Oh, God, get them off!*

I didn't know why I felt that way or what was happening to me. No one had ever said to me, "Don't worry if at times you feel dirty. It's a natural feeling after you've been raped." Oh, if someone had only told me, "It's okay. What you're feeling is part of the damage done to you." If only someone could have assured me, "It won't last forever. You'll get over it." If only someone had told me . . . if only someone knew . . . if only someone. . . .

11

As the weeks passed, Bob and I did discover the beauty of romance in our relationship. Although gradually I was able to find pleasure in our physical attraction to each other, the sentimentalism surrounding our first Christmas together made the sexual aspect of our relationship seem almost unimportant by comparison.

After spending Christmas Eve and Christmas Day at home with my family, I eagerly drove the seventy-five miles to Bob's house to spend a portion of the Christmas vacation with him. The twenty-seventh of December, 1969, was a special night that I will never allow to slip from my memory.

Bob and I had enjoyed a fireside dinner at a restaurant more elegant than was our custom. Upon returning home, we slipped quietly in the back door of his folks' house and down the stairs to the family room. There we savored every moment we had spent together that evening . . . the taste of fine food, the sweet perfume of roses in a silver vase, the glow of soft candlelight reflected in each other's eyes.

"Thank you, Robert. This has been the most beautiful evening of my life."

"The most beautiful? Of your life?"

"Yes, I can honestly say that."

"Good, because there's more."

"More?"

"Yes, I have something I want to give you." He reached in his pocket and pulled out a small gray box. As he handed it to me, he whispered, "With all my love."

Thirteen pearls surrounded a crest, a diamond in its center. His fraternity pin. My eyes blurred with tears.

"Robert, I . . . I don't know what to say . . . I—"

"Just say you'll wear it."

"Of course I'll wear it." I threw my arms around him and began to cry.

"All right. All right. Enough blubbering. I've been practicing on the curtains all day. Let me see if I can pin this thing on you."

It was our first commitment to each other. I could hardly wait to get back to school to share our good news with our friends. My roommate's screams, when she first noticed Bob's pin, brought several other friends out of their rooms. The news spread down the hall like a row of toppling dominoes.

Even the guys were excited for us. Two nights after we got back to school, Bob's fraternity brothers held a pinning ceremony. Bob and I stood outside the front door of my dorm as forty male voices serenaded us in three-part harmony. At the end of the ceremony, the president of the fraternity offered his good wishes and presented me with a bouquet of long-stemmed, pearl-white roses. I felt like a queen with a court full of attendants, my knight at my side.

This was the first identifiable turning point in my life after the rape. I was beginning to believe in Bob's love for me, to feel it as well as know it, and with this I regained some of my self-esteem and a sense of control over my own life. Yet, I was still in constant need of reassurances, feeling insecure and inadequate much of the time.

Another turning point occurred in the spring of that same school year, my sophomore year. With the help of my friend Jeanie, I was able to regain the self-confidence I had not known since before the rape.

―――――

I was sitting alone at my desk when I heard a knock at

the door. It was Jeanie, one of my newer friends, looking very serious. Even though we hadn't known each other long, I knew it was not like her to wear such a grave expression. In cloak-and-dagger manner she looked back around into the hall, then entered, closing the door behind her. As she spoke, she barely whispered.

"Now, Kay, I could really get into trouble for talking to you like this. It's about the Delta Phis. We had a meeting tonight after the tea, and a lot of us were really disappointed that you didn't show up tonight. Somebody said you went to the Alpha Phi event because you didn't think you could make it into the Delphis."

I had not gone through sorority rush as a freshman, but had decided to wait and rush as a sophomore. And what Jeanie said was true, although I was shocked that she was saying all this to me. When it came to doing what was right, Jeanie provided the standard to follow. I couldn't picture her ever breaking a rule. But what she was doing was strictly against all sorority rush regulations; the entire sorority could get fined for it. It was called "dirty rushing."

"I can't actually guarantee you a bid, but I'm willing to bet that you'll be voted in if you go to our last tea on Friday."

On our campus there were five local sororities, none of which held any national affiliation. The procedure was to attend all the sororities' events at the beginning of rush and then gradually narrow your choice to one at the very end. I had narrowed my choice to two, Alpha Phi and Delta Phi. Afraid that the Delphis would not accept me, my final choice had been the Alpha Phis, a group of humanitarian-type girls who were mainly concerned with societal and environmental issues. Although all the sororities had many attractive girls, Delta Phi was stereotyped as the beauty-queen sorority. They always had more representatives on the homecoming court than any of the others. They were also known to win the academic trophy fairly regularly, as they managed to keep their grade points high. This was the sorority to which Jeanie belonged. This was the sorority that wanted me as a member? I couldn't believe it!

I pictured in my mind the actives I knew and those

whom I had just recently met. . . . Jane was an attractive, brilliant student. Jan, tall and thin, was beautiful enough to be a model. Carol, a vivacious cheerleader, had been on the homecoming court. Every girl I thought of had so much going for her . . . good looks, talent, popularity, intelligence. And these were the girls who wanted me to join them, who felt I belonged? Jeanie was telling me so. Was it really true? Me? A rape victim, who out of total despair had nearly committed suicide just a few short months ago?

At that moment, Jeanie, unknowingly, had handed me the biggest vote of confidence possible. An attractive, intelligent, talented coed was telling me that's what *I* was. After all I had been through, I had been unable to see myself as anything but degraded, unwhole, dirty, and abused.

"It's your decision now. I've done what I felt I had to do." With that she left.

I held up my small hand mirror and stared at myself for a long time. My contacts made my eyes look even bluer than they naturally were. My long, dark blond hair was shiny and soft; my chubby-cheeked, baby-faced smile looked more womanly now. I was beginning to feel pretty, something I had not felt in nearly a year.

But more than that, I sensed something wonderful, really wonderful, rising up from deep inside of me. It made me want to run through a daisy field . . . stretch out my arms, look straight up into the blue sky, and turn around and around and around, breathing in the freshness of the air and drinking in every marvelous sensation surrounding me. . . . *I am a beautiful person again. I now can believe . . . I truly am . . . beautiful!*

At first, joining a sorority had not been all that important to me. I had decided to go through rush just for the fun of meeting new people. But I'm convinced that Jeanie's "dirty rush" and my ultimate acceptance as a Delphi helped immensely in my being able to go on with my life and move toward eventual acceptance of the rape. Bob had been telling me all along that I was special, but somehow I almost came to expect and even demand that from him. Not until I was able to see that other people also thought of me this way was I able to recover my image of self-worth that had been lost at the time of the rape.

Other incidents also contributed to the rebuilding of my self-esteem. I was asked to sing and play my guitar at the Coffee Grounds, a coffeehouse on campus, where I was well-received and asked back often. I not only heard, but inhaled every bit of applause offered. I also played guitar and led singing every Sunday evening for a high school youth group at one of the churches in town. Not only did I feel accepted there, but also needed and wanted. By the time I was a junior, my grades had moved from my lowest 1.7 semester to a 3.6 on a 4.0 scale. I had become very involved in my education classes and felt important and, again, needed in the second-grade class where I helped with reading. At the end of my junior year, I was voted a semi-finalist for May Day Queen.

In themselves, none of these would have been enough to bring healing; but when I put them all together, I could see a progression taking place. God was continually using the people around me to help in the rebuilding of my life. Day by day my self-respect was returning, my self-confidence was growing, and my self-worth as a vital, contributing person was surfacing to a point where even I could see it. I needed these affirming experiences. Some of them were bestowed upon me; others I sought myself. In combination, they helped to gradually lift me out of my periods of depression.

It was the beginning of my acceptance of the rape, but only a beginning. Other people had contributed toward the healing process, but further restoration would have to take place without their help. Together, Bob and I would have to face more pain.

12

I spent the summer following my sophomore year at Camp Manitoqua, this time serving as a full-time staff counselor. It was a rewarding time for me, and I experienced incredible personal and spiritual growth living in that environment. But when September drew near, I was anxious to return to school, and Bob.

After a summer of having to drive two hours just to see each other, it was good to be together again. During the year and a half Bob and I had been dating, we had done a lot of talking, and we had a favorite place in which to do it. There was a grade school not far from campus, and our special spot for problem-solving was at the end of the slide on the playground. Warm weather or cold, we would go there to make decisions or simply to be alone to share each other's day. We would reminisce about the good times we had spent together and dream about our future.

On our second night back at school, we returned there for a "slide talk." Bob sat down first at the end of the slide as he always did and then pulled me down in front of him, his arms around my waist. Relaxed and content, I laid my head on his shoulder.

"Doesn't it feel good to be back?" I asked.

"Sure does."

"It's almost like coming home to our home, isn't it?"

"Yes, Kay. We've built a lot of memories in this town."

"Not all of them good ones."

"No, but we've come out of it all loving each other an awful lot. And we've had our share of fun times, too."

"Like the time I planted clues all over town for you to follow to find your birthday present?"

"I still can't believe you put that one in the fish pond in the park . . . Kayleen . . . I . . . let's walk." We walked. First just outside of the playground and then around the block. I knew Bob had something on his mind; he had called me Kayleen. We came back to the slide, and he sat down and looked up at me. The expression on his face was difficult to interpret. I had not seen this one before.

I extended my hands to him and knelt down in front of him. "Robert, what is it?"

"Kayleen, I want you to be my wife."

"Oh, Robert, I want to be your wife."

Though to anyone else it may have appeared an unromantic setting for a proposal, for us there was no more fitting place. Here we had learned to communicate and solve problems together. Here the foundation of our relationship had been laid. And now here it was that our life commitment to each other had first been spoken.

These same words became the first two lines of our marriage vows exchanged a year later in August of 1971. We knew our first year of marriage would be difficult. We both had a year of school left before we would graduate. I would be doing my student teaching. Bob had some tough classes coming up and had been elected president of the student congress, which would involve a great deal of time and responsibility. But we were ready for marriage; we were deeply in love and solidly committed to each other.

With the blessing of both Bob's and my parents, we began making wedding plans even before Christmas. My mother and I finalized the details as our special day approached.

———

Bob called me at home on the morning of our wedding,

but we held to our promise not to see each other until the ceremony. Eventually, the moment came. Dressed in my white, Juliet-styled, floor-length wedding gown, I walked to the back of the long aisle and took my father's arm. Bob and his groomsmen were already standing at the front of the sanctuary. Our eyes met. I could not hold back the tears. I fought them the full length of the procession down the aisle. As I approached Bob, I could see that this special moment had brought tears to his eyes as well.

The promises we made to each other and to God in front of our families and friends were of primary significance, and we have repeated our wedding vows to each other every year on our anniversary to refresh and renew the commitment that binds us together. But the moment that speaks of the love God gave us to share for a lifetime was the moment in which we first saw each other, the moment in which I walked down the aisle toward Bob to join my life with his. It was a moment of purity, of magnificence. At that moment the gift of a new life was given . . . and received.

In this spirit our lives were joined. In this spirit we celebrated our union with friends and family at our reception. And in this spirit we came together on our wedding night, that moment for which it seemed we had waited forever.

We laid in bed together, realizing how much we belonged together, how right it felt to be naked and held so closely. But as Bob entered me, I felt pain, physical pain. . . . *No, God, not now. I don't want to hurt now. I thought it was supposed to feel good.*

The look on Bob's face revealed how wonderful it was for him. The joy of actually being inside me for the first time radiated from him. I began to loosen up and the pain lessened. *But, God, this isn't the first time I have hurt like this, is it? Roger Gray hurt me like this.*

Bob's words blocked out these thoughts as he spoke. "Kayleen, I love you so much."

"Oh, Robert, you know I love you. We're really married now, aren't we? This is really all happening, isn't it?"

"Yes, Kayleen . . . it's really all happening."

Roger Gray was in my thoughts only briefly that night,

but he was there long enough to change my mood from excited expectation to daylight reality. I delighted in pleasing Bob. And I was glad we had saved ourselves for each other on our wedding night. That much about it felt right and good. But thoughts of Roger Gray tarnished my own long-awaited joy.

Bob thought about the rape that night, too, but I didn't know it. Not until years later when I sat down to write about it did we discover what each of us was thinking that night. Bob said that he hadn't known what to expect from me the first time we had intercourse. He had even been afraid I might become hysterical.

Discovering each other's memories of that night was a somber realization for us both. We felt deeply saddened that we had to take more to bed with us on our wedding night . . . more than just each other.

13

Bob and I had spent a great deal of time together before we were married. As with any other couple, a fair amount of that time involved a physical expression of our love for each other, and most of it had been pleasurable for both of us. It had been difficult to save the physical union for our wedding night. We had fought the temptation many times.

The strong physical attraction we shared made it easy for me to deny my thoughts about the rape throughout our honeymoon and well into the early days of our lovemaking as husband and wife. However, in time my rape experience surfaced again in light of the new dimension in our relationship. When it happened, it came as a shock to both of us, for although we knew it would take time to become completely compatible, we found pleasure in our lovemaking.

We delighted in being married, in living together. Our first apartment was tiny, but it was *our* home. We had rented a two-bedroom apartment. One bedroom was only large enough to be used as a study; in the other we slept . . . we made love. . . .

"Oh, Bob, will I ever get used to having you as my husband? It's like a dream. I hope I never wake up."

"You mean you're not sick of me yet?"

"Sick of you? It hasn't even been two months. Besides, how could I ever be sick of you? Look at you, you hunk. I want to stay here in bed with you forever."

"Oh, Kayleen, it's so sensuous to be in the dark, just feeling you, loving you."

That night—that moment, suddenly, something happened. Terror arose within me. I couldn't suppress it.

"It's awfully dark in here, Bob. I can't see you."

"That's okay. Just hold me."

"I can't see your face." I could not control the horrible cinema of thoughts racing through my head. . . . *I want to see your face. Turn the light on, please. I have to see you. I have to know it's you. I can feel that it's you. It's your voice I hear, but I can't see you. Oh, please, turn on the light. Stop it! Please don't! Bob, it's you, isn't it? I know it is. But I can't see you. I have to be able to see you!*

"What's the matter?"

"Nothing."

"You're crying."

"I can't see you, Bob. I know it's you, but I can't see your face. Please. Stop! Leave me alone. I can't. I can't."

He got up, turned the hall light on, flung the sheet over me, and went into the bathroom. I was left alone with my tears, my pain. I had driven the man I loved from my bed because I couldn't see his face. Robbed of just one of my senses, all others were captured by fear.

Hearing my sobbing, Bob briskly returned to the bedroom.

"Get ahold of yourself!" He was yelling at me. I had become hysterical.

"I can't."

"Look at me. I'm your husband."

"I know . . . I can't."

"Stop it. You're out of control. Come back to me. I'm your husband. I love you."

"I can't . . . I can't."

"You can. You can. You can." He was shaking me by my shoulders. My head fell back, loosely resting on the tear-soaked sheet. I lay flat. Naked. Weak. The tears still streamed down my cheeks, but no strength was left to energize the sobbing. I became silent, still.

Bob lay next to me, staring at the ceiling. I wanted to reach for him, but I couldn't. I lay limp. Together we lay in silence, desperate to leave the moment behind us, but unable to do so.

He knew what had happened. I knew that he did. I felt my own pain coupled with his. Again, because of my anguish, he was forced to suffer with me . . . this time, intimately.

This was the first time the rape had affected our lovemaking, but there would be others. I discovered that I had suppressed a mountain of emotions regarding this thing called intercourse. The rape still had its hold on me. No longer able to fool myself or Bob, I realized that I had been unable to give myself completely to him.

I would start out uncontrollably turned-on. *Touch me. Bob, please touch me . . . but, Bob, I don't want to touch you. Not there. I will touch you anywhere, but don't make me touch that part of you. I don't even want to see that part of you. It's ugly. Don't make me look, and please don't put my hand there. I know it makes you feel good. I want to make you feel good. I want to give you the beautiful feelings you give me. I can't. I love you. I want you. I need you. But not that part of you. Oh, couldn't we just make love without that part? Just let me hold you . . . kiss you . . . feel you close to me.*

Oh, God, will it ever be right? Can I ever love all of you, Bob? I will try to make you believe I do. I don't want to hurt you. I don't want you to know that I just can't accept all of you. I will touch you there. But, please, get it over with. I don't like it. Will I ever like it? Will your penis always be something to get in the way of my enjoyment of you?

It's ugly like Roger Gray's. I never looked at his. His hurt me and left me devastated . . . violated. His stole dignity and wholeness and womanhood from me. And this thing that's attached to you, Bob. I know it's not his, but it's just like his. How can this ever be beautiful? How can this ever be right? Isn't there any other way to make love? Can't we make love without it? Why does it have to be this part of you that makes you feel so good, gives you such pleasure? And why do I have to be a part of that? Why do I have to be the one to make that happen for you?

Will I ever know how it's supposed to be . . . how it is for everyone else? We're newlyweds. It's supposed to be so wonderful. Oh, God, for me this has become the hardest part of being married.

I'm okay. Yes, I want you. I know I'm crying. I'm really all right. Don't stop. I'm just letting some feelings out. It's okay. I want you to feel good. I want to satisfy you. I want to give you that much. Please. Hurry. Oh, God, I want this to be over. I love you, Bob, but I can't show you the way I'm supposed to. I can't reach the covers. Please cover me up. I don't like being naked. Don't look at me. I want to get cleaned up. I feel so dirty. . . .

Can this ever be the wedding gift God gave us to share? Can it ever be good? Oh, God, will this ever be beautiful for us? Can healing extend far enough to reach into our bedroom? Oh, God, can it? Or will my rape always be the silent intruder? Will I ever feel okay again? I mean, completely okay?

Looking back on our lovemaking during the first year of our marriage, I wonder how we ever kept getting back in bed together. The passion of each moment may have started things, but it could only have been our solid commitment to each other that actually brought us through each time during this difficult period of adjustment. It took months for the intensity of the sexual trauma left by the rape to diminish, but it did, gradually, as we continued to give ourselves intimately to each other.

As Bob and I took control over the sexual aspect of the adjustment to my rape, room was left for still another step to be taken in the healing process. Bob and I had come a long way. Yet there was more. Something still had to be resolved between me and my God. This time Bob could not help.

14

By the end of our first year of marriage most of my rape experience had been put neatly on a shelf. I felt good about myself, about our marriage, and about life in general. I was my energetic, enthusiastic self again. Most of life was a celebration. Yet now and then an unresolved question surfaced—the question I had asked God three years before on the night I nearly took my own life. The following letter I wrote to God expresses my need for an answer to that question.

Dear God,

Remember me? I'm Kay. I committed my life to You at a church retreat when I was a sophomore in high school. I stayed close to You through my high school days even when it was tough to be different— to be a teenager and a Christian, too.

I chose a Christian college because I wanted You to be in the center of my life even when I moved away from home, from church, and from my Christian friends. At the end of my freshman year in college, I prayed to You, giving myself to You in service. In that prayer I asked You to take my summer and make it Your own. It was by *Your* leading that I went to the inner city of Chicago to work in Your church. I could have had my old job back at the jewelry store for another summer and made lots more money, but I chose to serve You instead.

What happened? I thought You wanted me there. That was *Your* work I was doing. It was by *Your* leading that I went there. Did You think that it was better for me to be raped and quit my job than to stay there the whole summer and work for You? I don't understand. It doesn't make sense. You don't still punish people today the way You did in the Old Testament times, do You? Jesus changed all that, I thought. You weren't punishing me, were You? I may make mistakes, but so does everybody else. Why should I deserve that? No, I can't believe You were punishing me. Why then?

Am I just an ungrateful, spoiled child? Should I be thankful to You that it was not much worse? I could have been beaten, stabbed, or raped again by all of Roger Gray's friends. I could have even been killed. Should I thank You instead of question You? Maybe I should. But somehow I can't help but wonder why You let any of it happen at all. You could have prevented it. You know I believe in Your miracles.

The words of Psalm 121 are still familiar to me, God. Do You remember how often I read them during my early days in the city? They were a daily comfort to me then . . .

The Lord is your keeper;
    the Lord is your shade on your right hand.
The sun shall not smite you by day,
    nor the moon by night.
The Lord will keep you from all evil;
    he will keep your life.
The Lord will keep your going out and
    your coming in from this time forth
        and for evermore.

What about that, God? Shouldn't I believe Your promises? I thought I was special to You. Did I read that wrong, or wasn't that a promise from You to protect me?

I just don't understand. Are You a loving God or are You a vengeful God? Did You have a reason for me to be raped? Did You really *want* that to happen to me? What reason could be good enough for that kind of pain? I nearly killed myself over it. Do You remember that?

I was only nineteen years old when it happened. God, that's a very young age to have to face that kind of crisis. I didn't even know what the beautiful, loving, sharing kind of sex was supposed to be like when all of a sudden I was violated in an ugly, twisted way. I was too young for that. I'm still too young to have been through this kind of suffering. All I have been through, Lord! I'm only twenty-two!

I just don't understand. Most of my life has been put back together now. The nightmares have been over for a long time. Bob and I enjoy each other sexually. I no longer go cold on him. I no longer get upset over violent TV shows exploiting rape. I no longer become nervous and paranoid when I find myself involved in a discussion about rape. Actually, I feel pretty together about the whole thing, except for You, God.

I can go about living my life normally now, except sometimes when I'm sitting in church . . . and I hear all those promises, and I am told that You are a compassionate God who not only loves, but also cares for His people . . . I just don't know what to believe. I just don't understand You, God. It doesn't make sense. I just don't understand.

———

Trying to understand God's will overwhelmed me. My frustration level raised, I finally went to my minister, hoping to find answers to my questions about God. Our conversation in his office helped a great deal, but it wasn't what was said there that ultimately changed my thinking about God. As I was leaving, Rev. Beyer handed me a copy of a sermon he had preached on a previous date dealing with the will of God. The message that came to me through that sermon changed my life completely.

God allows tragedy to take place in the world because He created man with a freedom to choose God's way or Satan's way. Why did God do that? Why did God allow evil to come into the world in the first place? Why did He allow that opportunity to be there? Why didn't He just make us to only love Him and love each other? And I ask . . . what would love be if one was not free to do otherwise? Love would be a hollow, empty experience. . . . God honored you and me by giving us a will. . . . If we could do no other than to love God, that love would be empty, void; our relationship would be nothing.

This explanation made sense to me. This much I could understand. It seemed rather simple. Because God had given me the freedom to choose His way, I had to recognize that He had given all of mankind that same freedom. Some, for whatever reason, would choose evil over good. One of those people was Roger Gray. Very simply, I had become a victim of Roger Gray's wrong choice.

But I still could not understand why He should allow this to happen to me. "But, God, why me?" It was through the same sermon that I found peace about this question.

The question, "How could God allow this to happen?" is best answered when we quit asking questions about God and go to Him in the midst of the tragedy, no matter how great, and trust Him to be the Good Shepherd who does not forsake His own. And it's there in His arms that somehow He brings meaning to us through it.

Several years ago I met a couple, in the first summer charge I had as a young pastor. They had been faithful members of the church until two years before, and I was told by the council to call on them. They seldom came out of their house, never came to church, and just seemed to be the saddest people around. I went to the home and introduced myself, and they invited me in. Sorrow was written all over their faces.

I said, "I understand you are members of the church, and I am glad about that. I am your pastor for the summer and wanted to get to know you."

The husband said, "Well, you'll never see me in that church."

I said, "Oh."

He said, "Yeah, we used to believe that God cared about us, but two years ago we got convinced that He doesn't. We had one son, just one. We loved him, and we raised him, and we gave him everything we knew. We gave him a Christian faith, and he loved God. And one day, coming home from a date, just outside of town, he missed a curve over there and wrapped himself around a tree, and he was killed instantly. Any God that treats me that way, I'll never love, and I'll never sit in His church."

Well, that's a pretty heavy issue for a young seminarian to walk in on. I didn't know what to say, and I just felt their sorrow and their pain and their grief and I didn't say, "I know how you feel," but I did say, "I'm feeling with you." And then it just flashed across my mind, so I shared it.

I said, "You know, God only had one Son, just like you. And He willingly gave that Son to die so that He could take upon Himself your pain, your sorrow, your shame, and provide an eternal life for your son, as well as yourselves."

And I said, "I don't know if that means anything to you this afternoon, but I share it for what it is."

And they looked at me and said, "We never looked at it that way before."

I said, "God loves you. God hasn't abandoned you. God cares about you."

And the man began to get big tears welling up in his eyes, and I said, "Why don't we just ask God to let that love bear upon us right here and right now," and I felt very much alive in God's Spirit and with His leading, and I took that heartbroken mother and that bruised, beat-up father in my arms, and I prayed with them, standing in the middle of that living room. I cried with them. And when we opened our eyes after the prayer, the mother was smiling and the father believed. And joy returned.

God was there all the time. They were just not allowing His love to do its great work in their lives. And when they did, it brought meaning to tragedy and hope out of despair. And they were back in church that next Sunday and continued to be there. They have a hope now. They have been comforted.

I can only explain it by saying they allowed God, who took the risk of creating a freedom that would allow for tragedy, to love them in the midst of it. Remember that no matter how tragic or painful the circumstances, no matter how brutally another's will seeks to destroy you or your loved ones, no matter how tragic the results of your own willfulness, remember, God is there, loving, reaching out, and caring for you. And as you allow Him to, you receive His blessing. . . .

What do we do when we don't understand God's answer? Are we to say, "God, you are unjust, maybe not righteous after all"? If we do that, then we remove ourselves from God's care; we wall ourselves out at the time of greatest need. We go through life cursing God and His people, rather than finding healing for our hearts, even if we cannot gain understanding for our heads.

What I can't resolve, I take to God and leave with Him. I trust Him. I trust that He knows best. And if I have been a victim of some horrible evil, then in the midst of that tragic need, I need the Shepherd's care more than any other time.

My eyes blurred with tears as I read that sermon. I was freshly moved by the story I had heard every Easter since I was a young child. In the light of my own suffering and the suffering of that couple, Jesus' death on the cross took on new meaning. God had *willingly* given His only Son, knowing He would die a horrible death at the hands of sinful men.

Even knowing He would bring victory out of evil, how God's heart must have broken when those He created and loved chose to crucify Jesus instead of believe in Him. How He must have suffered right along with His Son. How He must have grieved with that couple and felt their loss. And how He must have suffered with me over the pain of my rape and shared my anguish when I nearly took my life. Through the Cross, God entered my pain and made it His own.

––––––

Although I cannot always understand God's ways, I can trust Him. I cannot expect to be spared pain and suffering, but I can go to God in the midst of it and find comfort and love.

Because I can trust Him, I will never again need to ask the question, "Why me?" I am content to know that God's love is sufficient. In this I have found healing, a healing that cannot be found outside of His love.

People have said that being a rape victim must have been harder for me in some ways because I am a Christian. I say to them: I may have had tough questions to ask, but the joy in discovering His healing in the midst of such pain is a joy that can only be experienced by one who loves and trusts God. It is only through Him that there is healing. It is only through Him that my burden is lifted. It is only through Him that I find peace.

15

During my recovery from the rape, most of my anger was directed toward God for allowing the rape to happen. Because I blamed God, it was God I needed to forgive. Although God had done nothing wrong, in my mind He had. I had trusted Him enough to serve Him in the city, yet I was convinced He had forsaken me.

With the help of Rev. Beyer's sermon, I was able to return my trust to God, having learned that His grace is greater than any pain we must bear. In order to reach this point, I had to empty myself of anger and resentment, including that which I felt toward Roger Gray.

Although my life was no longer ruled by those emotions, there was still something wrong inside of me . . . something missing. The letter I wrote to Roger Gray (but never actually sent to him) reveals the essence of those feelings.

Roger Gray,
    You stole something from me, but I don't know what to call it. You left me with a feeling, a feeling I can't explain.
    It's as if when you raped me, you threw me into a deep, dark pit. I emerged naked. Piece by piece, I was able to retrieve my clothing. Sometimes I had to walk great distances to find the pieces, but I did find

them. The first item I had to recover was control over my own life. Then I found strength, self-confidence, dignity, and hope. I'm even discovering my own sexuality. I have found peace with my God. Yet, there was nothing I could put on that could make me feel like a complete woman. You must have taken a piece with you, Roger Gray. You see, a part of me was left naked. Inside of me, it felt like a hole, a hole that could never be filled . . . a vital part of me . . . stolen. Will I ever be a whole woman?

Why did the rape do this to me? Why do I feel like in that part of me called woman there is a vast emptiness? Roger Gray, I don't know how you accomplished that, but you did. I can look like a woman, I can act like a woman, I can do everything a woman does, but I can't feel like a woman. How did you take that from me, Roger Gray? I don't understand why I'm left with this chasm inside of me. Every other grown female seems like so much more of a woman. Sometimes I even get jealous of other women. They are whole, but I've been robbed. I look in the mirror, but I'm not all there. There's something missing. I can't explain it to anyone else. I don't understand it myself, but it's missing . . . gone . . . stolen. Will I ever find it? Must I always live with this hole inside of me? Can I never be a *woman*?

This was the final question. I don't believe I ever expected an answer when I asked it. I had come to accept the fact that the rape would leave me damaged forever in this area of my life. All else had been resolved. But since I had no idea how I might rid myself of that emptiness, I came to believe that it was something I would have to live with indefinitely. How could a person so mutilated ever become entirely whole? I believed it simply could not happen.

———

Bob and I worked for a year following college graduation to save enough money for him to go to law school. When Bob entered school, I was five months pregnant. The first semester was difficult for both of us. Law school was much tougher than college for Bob, and because our baby was due in January, I was no longer working. We had moved to Detroit and were now four hundred miles away from our parents. It was a lonely time for us, but I managed to keep busy typing Bob's papers, reading books, crocheting baby things, and getting the little nest ready.

By the time January arrived, I was filled to overflowing with anticipation. It was just a few days before my due date when I felt my first contraction. It came about six o'clock on a Friday night.

After thirty-six hours of contractions, with four and a half hours of hard labor, Carrie Ann Scott was born, all eight pounds and four ounces of her! I was exhausted but ecstatic. Our little Carrie was laid on a table near enough so Bob and I could both see her. She was crying up a storm. She had a hematoma on her head, bruises from the forceps, hair that stuck straight out, and the wrinkles of a newborn baby monkey. She was beautiful.

She was my child. Bob's child. God's child. A living, moving, breathing, crying, kicking, wonderful baby person. She had come from inside of me . . . me! I was just Kay Scott, but that floppy little baby on that table had just emerged from me!

After some minor repair work, I was wheeled back to my room in time to catch about an hour of sleep. When the breakfast trays came around at 7:30 A.M., I was awake. Awake and famished. I refrained from calling Bob (who had returned home) until about 8:30. Finally, I couldn't wait any longer. I dialed our number, and a very groggy, "What are you doing awake?" came from the other end of the line.

"Why should I be asleep? We just had a baby!" I felt wonderful. My exhaustion could not begin to cloud my excitement. I had never experienced such fullness of joy . . . such appreciation for life—mine, Bob's, and little Carrie's.

When the exhilaration of the morning had mellowed in the late afternoon, I still had no desire to sleep. Instead, I had an unrefusable urge to be alone with my thoughts. . . .
I am proud . . . I am beautiful . . . I am grateful . . . I am a

mother . . . I am a woman . . . oh, dear God, I am! I am a
woman! I am a whole woman! Look at me now. I am totally
free of you, Roger Gray. You no longer have a hold on me. Not
even you can take away this moment. Not even you. I am a
whole woman!

———

Looking back on the birth of our first child evokes many
emotions. I marvel at the miracle of life . . . how, by the
wonderful grace of God working between man and woman,
we are given such an incredible gift as life itself. It's overwhelming.

But for me, this gift meant even more. I would never
again feel that emptiness, that hole inside that I had been
left with after the rape. The birth of our child meant more
than motherhood to me. It meant womanhood. For the first
time I *felt* like the woman I was.

I find this all very hard to understand. Again I ask, why
did the rape make me feel as if I had been robbed of my
womanhood? And why had the birth of our child changed
all that? I don't have an answer to these questions.

And yet, I must ask one more question. What if, because
of the rape or for some other reason, I had been unable to
have children? Would I never have found that healing? My
history with God and the relationship we have had over the
years causes me to believe that had I not been able to have
children, He would have found another way to provide healing for that emptiness.[1]

———

God has given me motherhood . . . God has given me
womanhood . . . God has given me freedom . . . freedom to
enjoy His gifts.

He has given me Bob as a total person and myself as a

[1]Author's note: Other recovering victims who have struggled with issues
of womanhood or feeling feminine have found healing in different ways,
such as through vocations, counseling, and dating and marriage relationships. It is certainly not necessary to have a baby to be healed. This is
simply the way restoration occurred for me.

total person. He has given us our bodies.

There were days when even during our lovemaking I did not want to be naked. I did not want to see myself or to have Bob see me. Over the years, God has given me mirrors. At first it was difficult . . . but, oh, how beautiful it is now to be free to be naked and to even joyfully anticipate being naked. I am proud of who I am. I am a person who has been raped. Yet, I am a person who has been changed. The sky darkened, the winds came, and my house was blown away. But brick by brick, God and I and Bob have built a new home. And it's stronger and better and more beautiful than the old one could ever have been.

It was dark. I could see out the front window, and the street was quiet. I watched as the last light was turned off in the upstairs window of the house across the street. They were in bed. That's where I wanted to be . . . yet, not to sleep.

The fire was low, its only sound a crackle. Piercing the darkened room with its flicker, it fought to stay alive. Bob was stretched out on the floor. Asleep.

Lying down on the soft carpet next to him, I slowly ran my fingers up the back of his leg and moved them toward his hip. I could feel his body stir in response to my invitation. He was not yet awake, yet he was already feeling . . . and I was feeling.

As I touched him and brought him to me, his fingers began to reach as well. . . .

Together we give. Together we love. Together we enjoy. There are no tears of pain now. Any tears that come are an expression of the overwhelming joy we feel. We come so close to each other that we pass through and share oneness with each other and with God.

It did not happen suddenly. It has taken a long time. But I have the wings of a butterfly now. I have come from the ground, no longer crawling on the earth. I have grown to full beauty. I am free. I can fly. There is nothing to hold me back, nothing to pull me down. There is nothing I can't do, nothing I can't give. I can live and love in joy . . . in victory . . . I am free!

16

Ten Years After the Rape
(Written for the first edition of this book)

Bob went on to finish law school and is now successfully practicing law. During his first year as an attorney, we were again richly and joyfully blessed, this time with the birth of our son, Jeff. By the time Carrie was five and Jeff had reached the delightful age of two, I had begun to work on this book. Although Bob supported me in my writing from the beginning, he had decided he did not want to read any of it until it was completed. But one day, not too long after I had begun writing, his curiosity got the best of him.

It was Wednesday. He had slipped out early in the morning, not waking me or the kids. He wanted to get to work early so he could run off copies of my newest material for me before anyone else arrived at the office. I had placed the yellow, legal-sized pages in his briefcase the night before. On top of the pile was the section I had just finished writing entitled, "The Rape." As he stood in front of the copier, he suddenly realized what he held in his hands. It had been years since we had talked about my rape in detail. His curiosity was too much for him. *How does she handle the description of the rape itself? Did she write it all? Without being too graphic? How detailed is it?* He would take it back to his own office and just take a peek at what was there.

111

Alone in that small room, crowded with law books, his massive desk smothered in legal publications, files, and paperwork, Bob did not put the pages down until he had read all of it. By the time he called me at home a couple of hours later, he had calmed down some, but was still feeling emotions he hadn't known were there.

Suddenly it had become real to him from an entirely different perspective. At the time I was raped, Bob and I had only been dating for four months. We had made no commitment to each other . . . no fraternity pin, no ring. But now we had been married almost eight years. I was his wife, a dearly loved part of him, and Roger Gray had violated that. I could hear the rage singe through the inside of him as he uttered, "It makes me want to find that guy and. . . !"

At first I was confused by the fact that after ten years he still had such anger left. We talked about it after the kids were in bed that night. Not until then did I fully realize that most of what Bob had had to deal with at the time of my rape and soon thereafter was me, not the rape itself. He had spent most of his energies in helping me through it. He had never needed to deal directly with the rape, as I had. The details were not embedded in his mind. Now he was having to look directly at the rape, and it was painful.

In his mind, Bob was having to picture me, as his wife, with Roger Gray French-kissing me, squeezing my breasts, dragging me down the grimy stairs, pulling my underpants down, and inserting his ugly self into me. I had lived with the details replaying in my mind a thousand times until it was no longer painful, but just a memory. Bob had not. Now it was my turn to share in Bob's pain, and it hurt us both. We were able to work through it, as this kind of pain was not new to us, but oh, we wanted so desperately to close the door on the rape and leave it all behind.

Dealing with my total rape experience involved passing through a number of stages of recovery: shock, denial, anger, rationalization (I should be finished with it—let's go on as if it never happened), depression, and acceptance. One of the major points I want to make in this book is that past the acceptance stage, there comes another: the assimilation stage. This is when a rape victim can look herself straight in the eye and say, "I'm healed. I'm whole. I am myself. It's all over. I can go on with my life and leave the whole rape experience behind me completely. It's no longer a problem for me. I don't have to spend any more time with it. It's over." I want so desperately to be able to tell recovering rape victims and those who are trying to understand rape that this is all true—that there is a finality about it. But Bob's experience of reading the rape scene was a sober reminder that this would not be telling the whole truth. I have had to face the fact that the rape is something that will always be a part of me . . . something I cannot shove in the closet and shut the door on forever. A discussion I had with my minister convinced me of this.

It was through a sermon preached by my pastor, Rev. Welscott, that I first felt God leading me to write my story. When I decided to do it, I went to him and told him about it, seeking his support. Over the past two years, he has walked through all of the writing with me—reading each draft, offering advice, and helping me keep my perspective. One particular talk we had in his office lasted unusually long, nearly two hours, and I walked away from that meeting feeling somewhat confident about the road ahead. A couple of hours later, I nearly fell apart. I was confused, hurting, torn—feeling as if I would come unglued altogether.

We had talked, among other things, about signals. Most likely Roger Gray had given me some signals that could have clued me as to his intentions, but I missed them. He asked me to go to his "party." He followed me across the street. Who knows what else? We came from different backgrounds. We weren't speaking the same language. I was wearing my college windbreaker, labeling me an outsider. My sun-streaked hair was long and blowing in the wind. I was a female. I was alone. I said "Hi." I was sending out some signals as well.

Until this time, I hadn't allowed myself to feel guilt over the rape. I know from a year's experience as a volunteer with a rape crisis team that guilt is a normal thing for a rape victim to feel, whether she "has reason" to feel guilty or not. Now, what I am going to say next is very important: I am not taking any responsibility for the rape itself. I did not deserve to get raped. *No woman does, regardless of the circumstances.* I am merely taking responsibility for the fact that I missed some signals sent out to me and that I sent some signals myself. Taking even this small responsibility, however, made me feel guilty. It shouldn't have, but it did.

A mother sends her child to the store on his bike for a loaf of bread. On the way to the store, the child gets hit by a car. The mother feels guilty. "If I had gone to the store myself, this would never have happened." Maybe the child was riding no-handed in the middle of the street. Maybe the driver of the car ran a red light. It doesn't matter. The mother feels guilty no matter who was ultimately responsible. She shouldn't. But she does.

I felt this same kind of guilt. Though it's negative and painful, I think it's normal and healthy. It's an emotion that needs to be vented.

But this by itself was not what made me feel like I was falling apart. I had dealt with a lot more than this in the past. I could handle some guilt. What hurt was that I had convinced myself I had dealt with everything. Suddenly I began to dig into myself. I opened a door and found a skeleton I didn't know existed. I had been building up walls of protection for myself for years. A wall came down, and it hurt.

Although I had been able to say to myself in the past, *I am healed . . . I am whole,* at this point I had to say to myself: *You still have some healing to do. You have a problem to deal with here. Even though it has been put behind you, right now you hurt over this rape thing. Right now, ten years later.*

I want to have it over for good. I don't want it to touch me anymore—ever. I can't have that. I want it to be as if it never happened. I can't have that. I want to shut the door on it and never see the door opened again. I can't have that. This is the whole truth that, painfully, I had been hiding from myself.

My hope comes in knowing that though the past cannot be erased, it can be dealt with, and lived with, and then left behind. The past won't go away, but I can be healed. I can be normal. I can be whole. I can be myself. I am a different self than I was before. I have hurt, but I have grown through all my pain. The rape will never be completely gone from me. It will always be a part of me, but that's okay. I can live with that. It won't always hurt me. Only when I dig down deep inside of myself and reach and grab for everything that makes me, me—only then will I have to come face-to-face with that part of me again. And it will hurt, but that's okay, because it is a part of *me*. God did not make me a complicated being so I could be comfortable with myself. He made me the person I am so I can take the whole package—the suffering with the healing, the pain with the joy, the struggle with the peace—and be able to hold it all in my arms and look up at Him and say, "Thank you, God, for life."

Dear World,

Please treat me like the whole person I am. I laugh over Dr. Seuss stories with my two children, and once in a while I stumble over the words. I love to play racquetball and sometimes I lose. I do needlepoint or crochet in front of the TV and get frustrated when I have to rip out my mistakes. I love to make strawberry and blueberry jam, but I quickly tire of planning suppers. I go camping and hiking, and I can actually enjoy living in a tent for more than a week at a time, as long as the bathrooms have showers.

When I am already late for a dentist appointment and I have to wait for a freight train, I am quick to get uptight. I get depressed over silly little things when it's that time of the month. Injustices like child abuse and indifference to the world's poor upset me. I get teary-eyed at weddings and cry at funerals. I melt like a young lover when my husband picks out a sentimental card for my birthday. I get crabby when he has too many meetings.

I have two children, but I had three pregnancies. One ended in a miscarriage. Just because I suffered a rape does not make me exempt from other trials.

You see, I really am normal. I experience life the same way other people do. I am no more. I am no less. So please don't identify me with the rape every time I am low. Other circumstances are now the source of my struggles. And on the other hand, please don't expect me to constantly be on top of the world just because God has brought me through a very deep valley.

In most ways, I am like anyone else. So please don't treat me as if I'm dying if the cancer has been cured. And please don't expect me to soar like an eagle if I have the wings of a butterfly.

Kay

17

Twenty-Four Years After the Rape

Laughing over Dr. Seuss stories seems so far in the past, as do the years when my knees could withstand the pounding of a vigorous racquetball game. Quick-mix pans of brownies have long since replaced the dog days of home-made preserves. As a committed stay-at-home mom and volunteer, my never-ending challenges now include monitoring the revolving door of teenaged traffic in and out of our home and keeping gas in the "grocery-getter." My cupboard of unfinished cross-stitch projects sits neglected as I lavish my attention on sporting events, school functions, and church activities too numerous to calculate.

Over the years Bob has specialized in real estate law and running. In addition to numerous road races, he has run fifteen marathons, including two Boston Marathons. Together we have shared a full cup of life, and our love for each other grows deeper each passing year.

How grateful we are to have two beautiful children, now emerging into young adulthood. Recently we faced both the joy and the grief of a half-empty nest when Carrie departed for her freshman year at a Christian college three hundred miles from home. Jeff is an active high-schooler, and the precious time we have left with him at home will no doubt pass swiftly.

One of mid-life's imprints is the urge to reflect. It is a time of reaching back in order to gather wisdom and vision for the future. Reflecting on the past twelve years since my story was first published, I must conclude that I have lived the hope of every victim following her rape: a normal life. This is the bow on the package of healing, given to us by God.

Although I have rarely thought about my own rape during the past several years, I have steadily received letters and phone calls from victims of sexual violence. Sadly, although it is now more than two decades since my rape, many of the struggles victims face in recovery today are still the same as those I battled. Yes, we have made great strides in victim advocacy on the whole, but as a Christian community, we have a long way to go both in our attitudes toward victims and in providing the support they so desperately need.

The following pages of this book address the most frequently asked questions posed to me by victims, family members, friends, and professionals. While I do not claim to be an expert on sexual violence, my authority comes from my own experience and from what a listening ear has taught me.

In addition to these questions, many people have asked how and when we told our children about my rape. I can only answer this by saying it has never been any big secret. However, we did try to limit information in age-appropriate ways when approaching the subject. When Carrie and Jeff were small, we cautioned them about not talking to or going with strangers, as most parents do. At that time we told them that years ago I had been attacked by a man, that he had hurt me, and that we didn't want that to happen to them.

Sometime later we explained that the man who had attacked me had touched me in places I didn't want to be touched, and that this had made me feel bad inside. We explained that this would probably not happen to them, but that if it ever did, they should tell us, even if that person told them not to tell, and even if that person was someone we knew.

As they grew and gained knowledge about sexuality, we added details and answered questions as they arose, each time emphasizing that I was okay and that what had happened to me no longer hurts me. We always tried to be honest, without instilling fear or any hint of shame.

We have enjoyed both tender moments and laughter over this through the years. Once when Jeff was just learning to read, he pulled my book (previously titled *Raped*) off the shelf and innocently yelled from the living room into the kitchen, "Hey, Mom, why did you call your book 'Rapped'?"

Wrongful attitudes still bother me, but I now react to them as a victim advocate, not as a victim. Although I no longer feel the need to defend my own dignity, phrases like "for the rest of your life" and "for years and years" will quickly put me on the defensive, as they send dark messages to those in recovery. I will usually correct anyone using these phrases, explaining that victims of sexual violence should not be considered damaged for life. Unfortunately, when recovering victims hear people talk this way, they quickly lose hope, fearing they will always hurt the way they do in the initial stages of crisis.

To those of you who are victims in recovery, I would like to say to you: *hold on*. It won't always hurt this badly. You will make it. "For he who is in you is greater than he who is in the world" (1 John 4:4b). Although every emotion betrays the truth, the truth is that our God is faithful, and as you allow Him to, He will bring you out of the darkness. How do I know? Because I've been in the darkness. And so have many others who by the grace of God have also made it. You can, too.

PART TWO

Common Questions

18

Why Do They Blame Me?

Suppose Tom drives into Susan's driveway. He gets out of his car, walks to the door, and rings the bell. Susan answers the door and decides to invite him inside her home. He accepts her invitation and enters. An exchange has taken place; there is consent by both parties.

Sexual intercourse may be described in much the same way. In sexual intercourse, there is consent by both parties. There is an exchange taking place.

Rape isn't anything like this. Rape is an eighteen-wheeled semi-trailer truck barreling sixty miles an hour through Susan's living room picture window.

There is nothing pleasant or enjoyable about rape. Rape is not an act of sex. It is an act of violence. *Rape is not sex acted out aggressively. It is aggression acted out sexually.* It is by definition an act against the will. There is no exchange taking place. There is only "taking" taking place. The rapist steals what the victim has not given him permission to have. Rape is not entering by consent; it is breaking and entering by force, threat of force, or coercion.

Furthermore, rape is a violation of rights. We each have the right by law to walk down a city street and into a public apartment building without being raped, stabbed, shot, or harmed in any way. The man who raped me violated that

123

right, and when he did, he also violated every woman's right to walk safely on that street.

Was it wise for me to be there? Some would say no. Did I have an increased chance of being attacked because of the circumstances? Perhaps. But those who blame me for being there validate the rapist's right to own the street and invalidate my right to walk safely in that neighborhood. As a result, I become the one held responsible for the crime. Instead of Roger Gray (the perpetrator of the crime) being blamed, I (the victim) am being blamed.

If a drunk driver runs a red light and smashes into a young woman's car, is it her fault for driving down the street? Would it be her fault if she were driving down the street past a bar? Would it be her fault if she were driving down the street past a bar on New Year's Eve? No. *Regardless of the circumstances, even circumstances that might increase a person's chances of becoming a victim, it is the perpetrator who is responsible for the crime.*

When those close to the victim—family and friends—harbor an attitude of blame, the victim will feel unsupported by those she most expects to help her. Not only does this create a breakdown in their relationship, but she becomes less likely to seek help from others for fear of facing the same unsupportive attitude. Absorbing blame for both her own undeserved pain and the subsequent pain of those around her, she feels rejected, isolated, and helplessly alone. As a result, the pain inflicted by the rapist becomes compounded by the wounding attitudes of those closest to her.

In defense of parents, boyfriends, husbands, and friends, I must say that I believe, out of their own feelings of helplessness, many of them are really saying: "I wish this had never happened to you. I wish there was something that could have prevented this awful situation. Couldn't somebody have done something? Couldn't *you* have done something to prevent this horrible crisis we're all suffering?"

Yet, some believe if they can blame the victim, then they don't have to feel sorry for her or enter into her pain. Or, they may feel inadequate to help, and this attitude gets them off the hook. Others think she must have done something to ask for it. Otherwise they will be forced to believe it could happen to anyone, including themselves or someone else close to them. So they choose to blame the victim rather than face that fear. And many Christians find it easier to blame the victim than struggle with the theological issue of how a loving God could allow such suffering. If it's the victim's fault, then God does not have to be defended or explained. Still others are simply struggling to find answers.

Whatever the source of this attitude, it is one of the most hurtful things a victim faces. Wounds inflicted by an attitude of blame go deep—often deeper than the injury of the rape itself.

In *The National Women's Study* findings, as stated in "Rape in America: A Report to the Nation," victims who had been raped within the previous five years were asked: "Are you somewhat or extremely concerned about the following?"

- Contracting HIV/AIDS (40%)
- Contracting a sexually transmitted disease, not including HIV/AIDS (43%)
- Your name being made public by the news media (60%)
- Becoming pregnant (61%)
- People outside your family knowing you have been sexually assaulted (61%)
- Your family knowing you have been sexually assaulted (66%)
- People thinking it was your fault or that you were responsible (66%)[1]

It is clear from this study that rape victims are more likely to be afraid of the attitudes of their family, friends, and the general public than they are of contracting HIV/AIDS or other sexually transmitted diseases.

---

[1] The percentages in ( ) reflect the number concerned about each issue. "Rape in America: A Report to the Nation," April 23, 1992, prepared by: National Victim Center, 2111 Wilson Boulevard, Suite 300, Arlington, Virginia 22201, and the Crime Victims Research and Treatment Center, Department of Psychiatry and Behavioral Sciences, Medical University of South Carolina, Charleston, South Carolina 29425.

Only when we conquer the obstacle of blame and threat of blame will victims receive the necessary help for recovery. Furthermore, until attitudes change, victims will lack the courage to prosecute, juries will fail to convict, and rapists will go on raping.

19

What About Date Rape?

Victims of sexual assault are not chosen for their sexiness; they are chosen for their vulnerability. And who could possibly be more vulnerable than a young woman on a date? When trust is up, defenses are down.

A young woman named Sarah[1] shared her story with me four years after she had been raped. While she was in college, a young man had gotten drunk and raped her in his dorm room. To compound the horror, immediately after he was finished with her, he called several of his fraternity brothers into the room to show them what he had done.

As Sarah's story unfolded, it became evident that her rapist was more than a casual date. Sadly, this young man was her fiancé, and he had raped her just weeks before they were to be married.

After that horrendous night, Sarah canceled the wedding without ever telling anyone the real reason, not even her parents. Unfortunately, this meant that for four years she had carried the burden entirely alone. When she did finally share her story, tears flooded from her, and at times it was difficult for her to get the words out between the sobs.

Sarah never considered prosecuting. Even if she had

---

[1]Not her real name.

wanted to, who would believe her? Raped by her fiancé? The nice young man she intended to marry? Unlike any other crime, in the case of rape, victims are somehow made to feel they should have known better. Had Sarah been murdered by her fiancé, no doubt friends and family would have been shocked; but no one would have expected her to know ahead of time that he was a murderer.

Another reason victims like Sarah often do not report these crimes is *society's myth that rape is just sex that got a little out of hand.* On the contrary, as A. Nicholas Groth, a clinical psychologist who has studied both victims and offenders, explains: "Men don't commit rape to satisfy a sexual urge any more than an alcoholic drinks because he is thirsty." The rapist's motivation is a desire to dominate, humiliate, or get even. Rape is a violent act of aggression. It is one person overpowering and controlling another. It is devastatingly fearsome and horribly traumatic. Just because it happens on a date does not make it any less terrifying. In fact, a date rape may be even more terrifying because the rapist is someone the victim trusted, chose to be with, and possibly cared about or loved.

Although it is difficult to understand how anyone could rape his own fianceé, it is known that some rapists choose a convenient substitute for their true object of revenge. Although the rapist's aim is to dominate and humiliate, he does not necessarily hate the woman he is assaulting. In spite of the fact that most rapists plan their attacks, some are unable to describe the woman they have just raped, stating that it didn't matter who their victim was.

Statistics show that most date rapes occur on the offender's turf, such as in his hotel room, car, apartment, house, or area of town. This increases the victim's vulnerability and decreases the likelihood of her finding help to escape. Somehow society has come up with the mistaken idea that a woman voluntarily accompanying a man translates into: she has consented to whatever he wants to do to her. What a horrible, ridiculous conclusion. Just because I leave my jacket in your apartment does not give you the right to damage or destroy it; that jacket still belongs to me. Nor does a woman forfeit her right to personal safety just because she has dinner in a friend's apartment or accepts a ride home in his car or goes to an office party with him.

Regardless of whether it is date rape, acquaintance rape, stranger rape, gang rape, marital rape, same-sex rape, office rape, clergy rape, incest, non-familial sexual abuse, attempted rape, or any other type of sexual violence, we must stop blaming the victims.

Many choose to blame victims because they cannot believe rapes happen as they do. As victim advocates will tell you: "If you knew all the places rapes occur, you wouldn't go anywhere and you wouldn't stay home either." This is true for date rapes as well as rapes in general.

While serving on my local rape crisis team, I spoke with a young woman who was raped on the hood of a car in a restaurant parking lot in ten-degree weather. Another was raped in a snowbank in front of a store, just minutes after the store closed at nine o'clock at night. The store was located on a five-lane street near two busy malls. No one stopped to help her, probably because they couldn't believe their eyes. Most likely they thought it was just a young couple playing around in the snow. After all, no one would rape a woman as boldly as that. In another case, a jury had all the evidence needed to convict a rapist; instead, they acquitted him. Why? Because they just couldn't believe anyone would do something as horrible as the victim had described, and certainly not the well-dressed young man sitting in front of them.

In *Invisible Wounds: Becoming Streetwise About Sexual Assault*, Candace Walters addresses the issue of believing the victim:

> Every woman who decides to prosecute must undergo an extensive medical exam, a thorough interrogation by the police, and a detailed court testimony. One district attorney involved in hundreds of rape cases says it is nearly impossible for a false accusation to come to trial, and we should be more

concerned with protecting the victim's rights, not the rapist's.[2]

Both the boldness with which men rape and the audacity they display by what they do could be described as unbelievable, but until we start believing victims, rape will continue to be the most underreported violent crime in America. Whether or not the victim is on a date, in a man's apartment, hotel room, dorm room, or anywhere else—no matter the circumstances—*rape is rape.*

Most victims of date rape describe a Jekyll-and-Hyde personality change, where their attacker at first appears charming and then suddenly turns aggressive. Unfortunately, this makes the crime all the more unbelievable, since others may never witness the offender's violent behavior. And since the rapist uses the element of surprise to his advantage, it is less likely that he will use a gun, knife, or other weapon in the case of date rape. Instead, in addition to the shock factor, he uses verbal threats and physical force to overpower his victim.

Date and acquaintance rapes account for 60% to 80% of all reported rapes, but the true numbers are much higher than we know, since these victims are the least likely to report (for fear of being blamed). Also, 50% of the offenders in rapes of females under the age of eighteen are their boyfriends. "In many (date/acquaintance) cases a victim has been doing something either her friends or parents wouldn't approve of. She may believe that since she was breaking rules, she 'deserved' to be raped."[3]

Any victim of rape has a hard time with trust following an assault, but for the victim of date rape this can be especially difficult. Dating after an assault requires courage, and it usually takes at least some recovery before a victim

---

[2]Candace Walters, *Invisible Wounds: Becoming Streetwise About Sexual Assault* (Portland, Oregon: Multnomah Press, 1992).
[3]Date rapes tend to last longer and are most likely to occur on weekends between the hours of 10:00 P.M. and 2:00 A.M. Fifteen- to nineteen-year-olds are most vulnerable to these assaults. (Information provided by the YWCA Sexual Assault Center, 25 Sheldon Blvd., S.E., Grand Rapids, MI 49503.)

will even consider dating again. In order to have a sense of control over her circumstances, she may need to be the one to choose the restaurant or activity or set other parameters for a while. Also, it may be necessary for her to begin with daytime dates or double dates with friends she trusts. Although it will take time, her feelings of comfort, safety, and trust will return. Gentle encouragement and support from family and friends will not only help her be able to date again, but will also enable her to resume other normal activities.

20

What Can Family and Friends Do to Help?

Warm, concerned, loving communication from family and friends is crucial to a recovering victim of sexual violence, even if she seeks professional counseling. A counselor cannot replace these essential relationships. For, more than anyone else, it is those closest to a victim who influence how she will deal with the attack.[1]

The most important support you can offer is to insure truthful attitudes about sexual violence. Although you may not overtly blame the victim for her rape, she may sense otherwise by the way you interact with her during her recovery. And since your attitude will affect every communication you have with her, it is wise to engage in some self-examination. To determine whether or not you are thinking truthfully about what has taken place, ask yourself the following questions:

1. Are you frustrated or angry with her for bringing this crisis home?

2. Are you upset with her for all the police interviews, court appearances, counseling and/or medical

---

[1]Paraphrased from Washington, D.C. Rape Crisis Center Newsletter, March-April, 1973.

appointments that are disrupting your life and the life of your family?

3. Do you resent what she has cost you with her rape recovery expenses?

4. Are you judgmental because she has missed work, changed jobs, or dropped out of school due to her temporary emotional instability?

5. Are you annoyed with her because you've had to install locks, security devices, or even move to a different community so she can feel safe in her own home?

6. If the victim is your wife or girlfriend, do you get mad at her if she gets hysterical or goes cold on you during intimate moments?

7. If you are a friend of the victim, are you irritated with her because of her preoccupation with her own problems and her lack of focus on yours?

If these questions reflect the way you are feeling, then you are not alone. However, if you answered "yes" to any of these questions, then you will need to adjust your thinking. Not only is your support greatly diminished by these attitudes, but you are probably adding to the damage as well.

You do have a right to be annoyed, upset, and even angry about these situations. You do have a right to feel losses, for the damage extends to you as well. But it is necessary to realize that the victim is not responsible for any of this. It was the rapist, not the victim, who brought the crisis home. Similarly, she is not responsible for the disruption of your life, the need for added security measures, or any of your added expenses. All this is damage left by the rapist.

Also, although the victim is responsible for working toward recovery over time, she is not responsible for the devastating mountain of emotions the rapist has dumped on her. *Blaming her for the damage left by the rape is just as destructive as blaming her for the rape itself.* If you do not place the responsibility in the proper place—with the perpetrator of the crime—the person you wish to uphold will feel both blamed and unsupported.

These are just a few examples of the many situations in

which it will be important to separate the damage left by the rapist from the victim herself. Now, I encourage you to reread those questions, this time replacing the word "her" with "the rapist."

In each circumstance you face, it may help to ask two additional questions:

1. Would this be the situation if _____ had not been raped?

2. Who is responsible for both the rape and all of its subsequent damage?

As stated before, the answer to the second question is always "the perpetrator of the crime, the rapist."

If you have blamed the victim, directly or indirectly, then your relationship with her has been impaired and damaged. An apology for these wrongful attitudes may be necessary before the relationship can be restored. For it cannot be stressed enough that maintaining supportive communication with the victim is vitally important to her recovery.

Unfortunately, not only do relatives and friends tend to blame the victim, either knowingly or unknowingly, but most victims blame themselves in many of the same ways others do. For example, a victim may be afraid to prosecute for fear of "sending him to prison." You can help alleviate both fear and guilt by reminding her that the rapist will go to prison for what he did to her, not for what she did to him.

By examining your own attitudes and making adjustments where necessary, you will be able to reflect the truth to the person who has been victimized by the rape, thus becoming an invaluable support to her. If you should desire further help with this, your local sexual assault center can provide assistance. Remember, the emotional devastation is temporary. With proper support, the victim will recover.

Additional Practical Suggestions[2]

1. Initially, most women who have been raped do not react to the sexual aspects of the crime; they react to the

[2]Portions of this material were adapted from the Washington, D.C. Rape Crisis Center Newsletter, March-April, 1973.

terror and fear brought on by the attack. Many of those around her, however, particularly men, may find themselves concerned with the sexual aspects. The more this preoccupation is communicated to the woman, the more likely she is to have difficulties in dealing with her own feelings. Probably the best way to understand her feelings is to remember or imagine a situation where you felt powerless or afraid for your life. (See "How Do I Overcome the Fear?" p. 151.)

2. It is advisable for the victim to talk about the assault; however, it is not possible to generalize about how much she should be encouraged to talk about it. If a victim is in denial, pushing her to deal with it will only alienate her. More often the opposite may be true, as a victim may need to talk about her attack more than those around her think she should. It is important that you are not the one to set the parameters. It is best to let her determine how much or how little she needs to talk. You can be helpful by simply communicating your willingness to listen.

3. Specific questions are usually callous and unkind and not appreciated by the victim. Probing for details may only worsen the problems a victim may have in dealing with the assault. Instead, questions about how she feels now and what bothers her the most are more helpful.

4. Be aware of her fears concerning you. She may be afraid that you won't believe her, that you may tell others (police, family, friends), that you may insist she relive the attack verbally, that you will be judgmental, or that she may lose control or go to pieces in front of you. Deal with these issues openly. Take a risk by bringing them up.

5. Be willing to refer to a rape directly by saying the word "rape." If you are uncomfortable with this word, the victim will feel shame.

6. Do not convey that it is not okay to cry or that she should stop. Crying is a healthy way for her to release emotions.

7. Do not preach to her or insist that her assault was God's will. She may be angry or confused about her relationship with God. Instead, encourage her to talk about these feelings.

8. Because of your closeness to her, a victim may be more sensitive to your feelings. At times she may choose not to discuss her assault with you if she senses this will distress you. She may decide either to protect you from pain or to protect herself from having to deal with your emotions on top of her own. There may be occasions when it is advisable to relinquish your need to talk with her about it, in favor of directing her to someone else with whom she is more comfortable. You can still offer her your warmth, love, and acceptance and help her with other needs during these times.

9. Natural expressions of affection from those closest to a victim are often desired and needed. The absence of hugs can send a message that the victim is damaged or no longer lovable. However, during certain times in her recovery a victim may not be able to handle this physical contact. It is always best to precede the hug with, "Could I give you a hug?"

10. For those of you who may know the victim but may not be especially close to her, there are still ways you can be supportive. A blank face and silence is humiliating, as is small talk and avoiding the subject altogether. Let her know that you care about her by not being afraid to mention the rape. Not a lot needs to be said, but going on as if nothing has happened can be extremely uncomfortable for you both. Getting it out into the open will clear the air and allow your casual relationship to continue unmarred.

21

How Can I Support the Woman I Love?

Bob speaks to boyfriends and husbands:

What do you say to someone you love when she tells you she has been raped? I know now that saying such things as, "I understand," "Everything will be okay," or "It really doesn't matter to me" not only would have been dishonest, but would have trivialized Kay's pain and the immense trauma she was suffering. As an eighteen-year-old who had just finished his freshman year of college, I didn't realize all this, but somehow the Lord gave me the right words to assure her of my continued love, which was the one thing she really needed to hear.

Rape, unlike any other crime, leaves its victims feeling damaged and defiled in such a way that they no longer feel worthy of being loved. As boyfriends or husbands, it's not particularly important that we understand *why* our girlfriends or wives feel that way, but it is critical that we understand that *this is the way they feel*. And it is equally important that we do not try to deny them those feelings by telling them that things really aren't so bad and that they have no reason for feeling that way. Quite simply, rape victims feel unlovable, and telling them they shouldn't feel this way only confirms their conclusion that something is wrong with them.

Being a part of Kay's recovery from rape has made me painfully aware of the important role a boyfriend or husband can play in that process. Too often, however, we just want it to be over, to put it all behind us and get on with our lives. *After all,* we think, *I've assured her that it doesn't make a difference in how I feel about her. Why is it still a problem?* What we fail to recognize is that it will continue to be a "problem" until the fact that she was raped no longer makes a difference in how *she* feels about herself. And, as Kay has described, that can be a long, slow process requiring a great deal of patience on our part.

In many ways, dealing with a loved one's recovery from rape can be much more difficult than accepting the fact of the rape itself. Our rational minds tell us that it wasn't her fault and that she did nothing to deserve what has happened. We tell ourselves that it is over and there is nothing we can do to change what has occurred. However, accepting and dealing with the aftermath is another matter.

With Kay, I so desperately wanted everything to be "normal" again. As a result, I was often content with those periods when she was in denial and readily accepted her assurances that she was all right. In fact, I am sure that there were times when my inability to contend with the ups and downs of Kay's recovery caused her to suppress her feelings and fall back into denial, just to save me the continued frustration and anguish of dealing with her emotions. Of course, each time that happened, her recovery process came to a screeching halt. In fact, it took a step backward as Kay assumed responsibility for my pain.

What can we do to help rather than hinder recovery? Of utmost importance is learning to lean on God for strength and patience, since a lot of both will be needed during the recovery process. Boyfriends and husbands also need to accept their roles as caring listeners and comforters within a larger support system that, hopefully, will include a professional counselor, a pastor, family, other friends, and possibly even a support group. *While we may want desperately to solve the problem for her, we can't.* Within her support structure she will need to find the answers for herself as she begins to regain control over her life and reestablishes her feelings of self-worth. Much of the time, all we can do is be facilitators, providing stability and a safe haven, along with regular expressions of love and caring through both word and deed, while she searches for those answers. Expressions of your acceptance of what has happened are also very important.

Not long after Kay and I returned to college, she seemed to have an overwhelming need to talk to people about her experience. Telling others was a necessary part of Kay's processing her feelings as she struggled to understand and accept what had happened. However, that need also arose from her desire to find someone who truly understood what she had been through and who could provide hope that she would not always hurt so badly. She needed to find some assurance that someday she would feel okay again. Unfortunately, at that time, without organized rape crisis teams or other victims willing to speak out, the most Kay found was someone to listen.

Although I wanted her to find those who could and would provide the understanding and hope she needed, I often felt uncomfortable with the thought of so many other people knowing that my girlfriend had been raped. The only person I told at that time was my roommate. I didn't even tell my parents until shortly after Kay and I were married. My explanation, of course, was that what had happened was really no one else's business and that telling anyone who didn't need to know not only risked affecting how others thought of her, but also could lead to rumors and gossip. However, I have since come to realize that my attitude also conveyed the not-so-subtle message that I was ashamed of what had happened.

So, my advice to you is to work at overcoming your feelings of discomfort with talking about your girlfriend's or wife's rape: first, by being willing to discuss it openly and honestly with her, and then, if she agrees, by being willing to discuss it with others. These assurances that you do not attach shame to her will not only help restore her self-esteem but will serve as an example for others, who will then be less likely to place shame where it does not belong.

Some care must be taken, however, as to how you express your feelings about the rape. For example, anger that places responsibility on the rapist can show how much you care about what has happened and validate your girlfriend's or wife's own feelings. But any anger directed toward her will only add to her trauma and undermine her recovery. Moreover, anger and hurt expressed too intensely may increase her own feelings of guilt as she accepts responsibility for the pain that has been inflicted on the man she loves.

At this point, because of the delicate balance required, it may be helpful for you to seek your own support system as an avenue for venting your frustrations, anger, and pain. This group may include some of the same people supporting your girlfriend or wife, but may also involve other close friends or the loved ones of other rape victims.

As I reflect on Kay's recovery, I can only regret that the help available today was not available then. Having support systems for both people significantly reduces the amount of time the couple needs to spend together dealing with the rape. Struggling with tough issues can, with God's help, bring two people closer together, but spending too much time at it simply wears you out and becomes counterproductive.

Finally, a boyfriend or husband can serve as a much-needed measuring rod, pointing out the progress their loved one has made in her recovery. This is particularly true during the low points, when she is so wrapped up in how she feels at that moment that she loses perspective on where she is in the process.

Recovery from rape requires dedication, perseverance, and a long-term commitment from a couple. But, as Kay has stated so clearly, the relationship God can build in this process can be stronger and more fulfilling, making the couple better equipped to deal with the rest of their life together.

———

As Bob and I worked through the tough issues during my recovery, we discovered (often the hard way) that sometimes when I expressed discouragement or frustration in the form of a question, there was an underlying message longing to be heard. Because so often I could not define my own need, he was helpless to know how to respond. With Bob's assistance I have written the following, hoping to provide a window into the needs of the recovering victim.

Beneath What I Say

Will I ever be all right?
Please look beyond the damage and offer your unconditional acceptance.

Will I ever stop feeling afraid?
Please hold my hand in the dark, but only until I can stand alone.

Will I ever get rid of the anger and hate?
Please remind me that these emotions are not the real me, just a part of the load on my back.

Will I always feel so helpless?
Please don't tell me what I should do. Instead, help me explore the alternatives so I can decide for myself.

Will I ever be able to trust again?
Please encourage me to take risks, one small step at a time.

Will I ever be healed?
Please help me see my own progress, as some days it feels as if there's none.

Will I ever regain control of my life?
Please don't do things for me that I can do for myself.

Will I always feel so alone?
Please don't try to solve it. Just be here to listen.

Doesn't anyone understand?
Please don't tell me I shouldn't feel the way I do. Just allow me to express the feelings I have.

Will I ever be able to love and be loved?
*Please help me feel special through your eyes until
I can see with my own.*

Will I ever be finished with all of this pain?
*Please remind me that it won't always hurt and en-
courage me to continue to heal.*

Will I ever find peace?
*Please gently point me toward Jesus and toward the
foot of His cross.*

And when the victory has been won, my friend, you will
be counted among the greatest of treasures.

22

How Do I Overcome the Fear?

I don't believe I have ever met a victim who was only afraid of being raped during her assault. Most are afraid they are also going to be physically brutalized or killed. Initially, following an assault, many victims express relief that they are still alive.

With or without a visible weapon, a rapist uses the power of coercion—threats, intimidation, and/or physical force—to overcome his victim. He also instills shock by using the element of surprise. One moment he may appear as normal as anyone else, then suddenly and boldly he attacks like a savage animal.

The intense terror brought on by sexual assault often causes a victim to do or say things that may later be interpreted as participation. For instance, when the man who had just raped me kissed me out on the street, I put my arms around him, accepting humiliation as a small price to pay for my life and Rev's. Sometimes victims remove articles of clothing or assist the rapist in other ways, complying only to save their lives. Some victims try complimentary or pleasing conversation, hoping this might soften the rapist and cause him to stop the attack. If a victim does not fight back or scream during an attack, it is most likely because she fears for her life. At first shocked by the attacker's abhorrent behavior, she then becomes terrified by the thoughts of what he might do before he is through with her.

The power that the rapist has over the victim is instilling terror. She responds both to the terror and to the power he has over her by doing whatever is necessary to survive the attack. Yet sadly, and far too often, the rape victim is blamed for "participating," rather than commended for doing what was necessary to survive.

This terror does not end when the attack is over. Fearing retaliation, some victims don't report the assault immediately. Unfortunately, police and jurors often question whether a rape has even occurred based on this delay, rather than acknowledging the power of a rapist to instill fear for one's life. Also, during court proceedings a victim will often be more afraid of seeing the rapist again than she is of having to tell her story. It is not unusual, in fact, for a victim to fear her rapist's return even beyond the initial stages of recovery. She is afraid that he will be able to get to her.

In addition, following an act of sexual violence a victim experiences a loss of innocence. She now knows she is not immune from horrible things happening to her. Often the result of this realization is unbearable, overwhelming fear. Knowing anything can happen at any moment beyond her control, she may not only fear further rape or her own death, but she may also fear (either for herself or for others) any other hardship that can occur.

It is not surprising, then, that following an assault, "How do I overcome the fear?" is one of the most frequently asked questions. It has been said that "courage is not the absence of fear but the conquering of fear." If you have been victimized by rape, then learning to conquer fear will be an important part of your recovery.

Anyone hoping to move the whole mountain in a moment, however, fails to recognize that recovery is a process. To begin, I suggest *breaking fear down by identifying specific fears*. The following list represents many of the common fears that follow victimization:

1. *Fear of men.* Victims may generalize by attaching

fears and suspicions to all men, or their fears may be limited to men with characteristics that remind them of their attacker. (For example, all men with mustaches, etc.)

2. *Fear of retaliation from the offender.* This fear is especially apparent in victims who decide to press charges. Any actual threats of retaliation should be reported to the authorities; restraining orders can be issued if needed.

3. *Fear of facing the offender, especially unexpectedly.* If she knows him and is likely to encounter him where she lives, works, or goes to school, this fear can be particularly prevalent.

4. *Afraid to trust.* This fear may invade any relationship and may be far-reaching, but it is most evident when a victim who is single begins to date again.

5. *Fear of reactions from family and friends.* The victim needs as much support as she can get in order to recover, and she may be worried that she won't receive it. Although it's not unusual for her to underestimate her support, she may choose not to tell others about her attack for fear of how they may handle the crisis. She may be afraid that she won't be believed or that she will be blamed for what has happened. She may be afraid a relative will take the law into his or her own hands and go after the rapist, or any of a number of other reactions.

6. *Fear that confidentiality will be broken.* This piggybacks off her being afraid to trust. She may fear confidences will be broken by family, friends, co-workers, police and hospital personnel, the media, and even counselors. If verbal assurances are not offered, she may need to ask for them.

7. *Fear of becoming pregnant.* Even though pregnancy as a result of rape is rare, a victim fears she will become the rare statistic. Even if told she's unlikely to become pregnant, she will probably entertain anxious thoughts.

8. *Fear of AIDS and other sexually transmitted diseases.* This fear extends beyond the victim herself to include the health of her partner and future children.

9. *Fear of the anniversary of the attack.* Associating the event with the date, it is common for a victim to need support within a week or so before the first anniversary of the

assault. This can be especially difficult for those who are victimized on or near a holiday—a time when everyone else celebrates. With much of her recovery behind her, she is afraid she will relive all the pain and lose control of her emotions. As she grieves a whole year's losses and assesses all the damage, she fears she will not be able to cope with whatever the day's memories may bring. Often the anticipation of the anniversary is more traumatic than the anniversary itself, and the first year is usually the toughest. Eventually, the anniversary will bring only a brief moment of sadness, and some years she may even pass the date without thinking about the attack at all.

10. *Fear of sexual dysfunction.* The victim may fear isolated incidents of "going cold" or becoming hysterical. If she is without a partner, she may worry that she will never be sexually desirable or able to love freely.

11. *Fear of being alone.* She may fear being alone at home, at work, in the car, at church, or other places. This will be most acute in the initial stages of recovery.

12. *Other fears based on circumstances.* Fears are varied and sometimes relate to the circumstances of the assault itself. Although those who have not been victimized may share these same fears, a victim of sexual violence will most likely experience a heightened intensity of emotion as a result of the sexual violence. A few of the common ones are: fear of going places alone at night (especially if she anticipates parking in a dark parking lot or ramp), fear of answering the door or phone, fear of repairmen working in or near the home, fear of staying in hotels or motels, and fear of traveling outside a self-determined comfort zone.[1]

Once a victim has identified specific fears, she is ready to get about the business of conquering them. With taking back control of her life as a primary goal, the recovering victim will first need to learn how to manage her fears and

[1]Portions provided by the YWCA Sexual Assault Center, Grand Rapids, Michigan, as adapted from " 'Friends' Raping Friends: Could It Happen to You?" by O'Gorman-Hughes and Sandler for the Project on the Status and Education of Women, Association of American Colleges, Washington, D.C.

then eventually how to overcome them. She will quickly notice that fear is a complex emotion with varying degrees of intensity.

I like to visualize fear as a ladder. On the top rung is terror for one's life. Terror shocks, incapacitates, and screams, "In the next few seconds you could die." The descending steps are intense fear, fear, high-level anxiety, worry, low-level anxiety, and, finally, comfortable level ground. The object of the victim in recovery is to climb down the ladder, one step at a time, until she reaches the comfort zone where she can once again feel safe. As she gains experience in this process, she will discover that she nearly always has alternatives, which means she will no longer need to feel victimized by her circumstances.

For example, if she fears staying in hotels, she may inquire about the hotel's security measures when she calls for a reservation. She can ask about dead-bolt locks on the doors, locks on sliding glass doors and windows, and security measures for outside entrances. Of course it helps to travel with someone, but if she must travel alone, she may pay a little extra for double occupancy and make her reservation as "Mr. and Mrs.," whether or not she is married. She may prefer to stay in motels with inside hallways, and when she checks in, she can ask for all the available keys (or key cards) to her room. She may also carry mace on a key ring (or in her suitcase during airline travel, since flight regulations prohibit passengers from carrying mace aboard on their person). One person may prefer to sleep with a television or radio on; another may feel safer when it's quiet.

If she has thought through and implemented precautions like these ahead of time, the recovering victim may be able to approach her hotel room with only low-level anxiety rather than intense fear. In any case, attending to these measures will significantly reduce her level of fear. The more often she stays in hotels, the more at ease she will become with them.

Although what makes us feel safe varies from person to person, it is important to realize that we do have options.

Depending upon the situation, some precautions may become permanent, but others may only be necessary until some level of trust and comfort is restored. The main objective is to feel as safe as possible while trying to regain normal activities. Local sexual assault centers can offer further assistance as the recovering victim explores options and seeks to regain control over various areas of her life. It always helps to talk through fears with someone who can offer nonjudgmental support.

After identifying a specific fear and exploring and implementing alternatives, a victim may still find herself dealing with an unmanageable level of fear. That was certainly true for me a little over a year ago when a rapist terrorized our neighborhood. We live in a normally low-crime area of town, but over a short period of time there had been numerous break-ins and two brutal rapes. Six of the break-ins were within two blocks of our house, and one of the rapes had occurred just a few houses down on the street behind us. The other rape occurred about a mile from our house. In the latter case, the victim was eighty-one years old. Her husband was at home when it happened, and he was brutally beaten by the rapist.

Needless to say, everyone in our neighborhood was frightened. Some of our neighbors even went out and bought dogs. As experience had taught me, I began to do everything I could to descend the ladder of fear. I went to neighborhood watch meetings, where I learned that the entire police force was working extra shifts in order to catch this criminal. During one of these meetings it was mentioned that the offender's M.O. was to take the first available phone off the hook as soon as he broke into the house. Then he'd go find his victim. So when we went to bed at night, I unplugged the kitchen phone and took it upstairs. We also reminded our children of the 911 procedure and talked through alternatives, trying to resolve as many "what-ifs" as possible.

When we discovered that the offender's route was likely to be right down our street, many of us sat at our windows at night, on the lookout for any suspicious activities. One of the first nights I did this, I noticed a pickup truck circle the block several times. When I called the police to report this, I was relieved to learn it was a plainclothes policeman patrolling the area in his own vehicle.

Doing all these things helped to reduce the intensity of fear, but we still had to go to bed at night and try to sleep. This was not like other situations I had worked through in the past. It was not just a "maybe it could happen" kind of a situation. There was a known danger at hand, for our family and our neighbors.

As I sat looking out the window night after night, I came to realize there was nothing more I could do to feel safe, short of leaving our home. Who knew whether this rapist would return or whether the police would ever catch him? It was at this point that I reached a decision: I made a conscious choice not to let this rapist have the power of fear over me. His evil power was robbing me of sleep and disrupting our normal family life.

Making the decision to let go of my fear was important, but this alone did not solve the problem. Because once I gave up my fear, I had a tendency to take it back again. So I not only had to let go of my fear, but I also had to let God take it away. I had to set my ladder of fear at the feet of the Lord, then turn around and walk away.

As I did this, I once again discovered something beautiful about our Lord: He never lets us go away empty-handed. For it is only after our hands are emptied that we can hold His perfect package of peace. After that, when the tendency to become afraid resurfaced, I reminded myself that I had given it to God and that He was the keeper of my fear. As a result, I was able to cautiously resume my normal activities and sleep peacefully. Without fear.

Some who read this may not understand that previous paragraph. Only one who knows God can appreciate the mystery of His peace. In Philippians 4:6–7 it says: "Do not be anxious about anything, but in everything, by prayer and petition, with thanksgiving, present your requests to God. And the peace of God, which transcends all understanding, will guard your hearts and your minds in Christ Jesus"

(NIV). His peace cannot be explained in human terms. It can only be experienced through the power of the Holy Spirit. His ways are not our ways, and they are beyond our understanding and explanation. As I let go of my fear that night, giving it to the Lord, I still did not know whether the rapist terrorizing our neighborhood would break into our house next. But I did know that God is sovereign over everything. Everything. That was all I needed to know. As I allowed Him to reign in my life, I knew that no matter what happened to me or to my family, He would bring victory. His peace conquered my fear because His power is greater than any evil power on earth.

A word of caution is necessary here, however. Pastors and other well-meaning Christians sometimes think they are helping victims of sexual violence by suggesting that they should simply "give it all up to God" and get on with their lives. Such advice is totally inappropriate. Nothing will drive a recovering victim away from the church faster than a comment like this one. It is best to meet the victim where she is, not where you think she should be. Only then will she be able to move forward.

If a rapist had been terrorizing our neighborhood right after I had been raped, no doubt I would have found another place to stay until the crisis had passed. I would not have been able to simply give it to God, because I would not have been ready to trust Him at that point. A certain amount of recovery needs to take place before that can happen, and the timing will be different with each person. The recovering victim needs to spend time regaining control over her own life, the very control her rapist has stolen from her, before she is ready to entrust anyone else, including God, with her life again.

I assure you, the strength you see in my recovery is not my own. It is a testimony to the incredible power of God available to each of us to conquer evil in our lives.

God wants to take from you whatever is weighing you down and replace it with the gift of His eternal blessings, not the least of which is His peace. I challenge you to spend time alone with the Lord today, placing your burden before

Him. Don't put it off another day. However, if you are just not able to trust Him yet, don't despair. On that day when you are ready, He will be waiting for you with open arms.

The man who terrorized our neighborhood was eventually caught and is now serving a life sentence. At the time of this incident, I asked God in prayer, "Lord, what good can ever come from all of this?" That's a question many of us ask when hardship strikes our lives. Yet, by identifying specific fears, exploring and implementing alternatives, making a conscious choice not to let the power of evil reign over us, and, most importantly, by giving our fears to God, we can walk away from events like this as conquerors of evil. As children of God and joint heirs with Christ, we have a tremendous source of power, strength, and peace that no one else can know. Praise be to Him.

23

When I Pray, Why Do I Feel Like God's Not There?

Like many other victims of sexual violence, I felt separated from God following my rape, particularly when I tried to pray. With a mountain of negative emotions weighing me down, I wondered: *Why does God seem so far away? Is He withholding His love from me? If God could raise Jesus from the dead, why can't He make me feel better? Why can't He just make it all go away?*

When grief from a traumatic event overshadows us, we may question the very presence of God in our lives. Blinded by our losses, we neither feel nor see the favor of God. We are told that if we cannot sense His goodness, then we must trust Him. But we *did* trust Him to take care of us. And yet He allowed us to become victims of this terrible evil. Trusting Him just isn't that simple anymore.

Following sexual violence, or any traumatic event for that matter, our relationship with God changes. We are no longer sure exactly who He is in light of our recent suffering. Nothing can alter the fact that the event has occurred. We can only change how we will deal with what has happened. Essentially, we have two choices. We can either go through the crisis with Him, or we can go through it without Him.

Unfortunately, instead of examining *how* to pray in the

midst of suffering, many victims choose to abandon prayer following an assault. Yet, as Rev. Beyer's sermon stated, this is a time when we need the Shepherd's care more than any other time in our lives.

I did not see God working until I had healed enough to detect His hand in my recovery. Unfortunately, for me, this came in retrospect and a long way into the healing process. It doesn't have to be this way for everyone. With specific, obedient prayer a victim can sense the powerful presence of God early in the process and throughout recovery.

Like many others, I needed to learn how to pray. As a member of Bible Study Fellowship some years later, I was taught by wise leaders how to make specific prayer requests. Below, I have listed some examples, showing the difference between nonspecific and specific prayers.

Nonspecific: Please help me today as I go to court.

Specific: Please . . .

1. Replace my fear with courage to face the man who attacked me.

2. Replace my nervousness with calm enough to speak clearly.

3. Provide wisdom as to how to answer their questions.

4. Give me strength enough to persevere if I should break down.

5. Open the minds and hearts of the people who will hear testimony today. Give them wisdom and help them to discern the truth.

6. Give me (and those going with me) the power to cope with whatever surprises may occur.

Nonspecific: Please help our relationship (marriage, parent/child, boyfriend/girlfriend, friendship) to improve.

Specific: Please . . .

1. Place a desire in each of us to work toward healing this week.

2. Provide the opportunity for [Bob] and me to talk.

3. Give each of us the patience to be good listeners.

4. Help us to sort out the truth from the lies Satan would have us believe.

5. Replace our discouragement with hope.

6. Help me to release my anger today in ways that do not create more damage.

7. Help me to be conscious of [Bob's] needs as well as my own.

8. Provide people to uphold [Bob] during this time when my needs are so great.

9. Provide me with another person who will listen, so [Bob] doesn't become so weary.

Praying specifically not only helps you define your needs and the needs of others, but also means answers to prayer will become tangible. I strongly suggest that you keep a prayer journal and date each entry, thus providing a way to monitor your own progress. When you do, you will begin to see God working in ways you never could have imagined. Numerous times I have stood in awe of the way God has answered prayers, many of which I had even forgotten I had prayed until I looked back through my prayer journal.

Your first entry may need to be, "Please give me the desire to keep a journal, and help me to find the discipline to stay with it." Or, it may be, "I'm so angry with you, God, I'm not even sure you are there for me. So please replace my disappointment in you with a desire to try to communicate with you."

Regardless of where you are, the important thing is to begin, whether or not you *feel* like praying. We do not have to feel reverent. God can handle our feelings, whatever they are, and He welcomes us even if we come shaking our fist at Him. The important thing is that we come to Him.

There is a plaque hanging in the office of my former pastor, Dick Welscott, that reads, "The difference between a hardship and an opportunity is the attitude you take toward it." Every tragedy provides the opportunity to know God better. He has not left you. Please don't be the one to leave Him just because your circumstances have become impossible. In time, if you allow Him, He will show you He is Lord over all, and His specialty is the impossible.

There is much more I could say about this subject, but with so many good books available on prayer, I will defer to them. I do encourage you to work on your prayer life by reading at least one book on prayer. For, even more important than finding solutions to our problems, it is in prayer that we come to truly know God and to know Him intimately.

Too Busy Not to Pray by Bill Hybels is a book that has helped me grow in my own prayer life.

"The greatest fulfillment in my prayer life has not been the list of miraculous answers to prayers I have received," writes Hybels, "although that has been wonderful. The greatest thrill has been the qualitative difference in my relationship with God."[1]

Hybels uses a format called ACTS, which means balancing each prayer with Adoration, Confession, Thanksgiving, and Supplication. When I adopted this pattern for my own prayer life, I found an intimacy with God I had never known. God doesn't want just a shopping list of our needs and wants; He wants us to *know* Him.

You may find it difficult to begin your prayers with adoration in the early stages of recovery, since it's likely you don't *feel* adoration for God much of the time. Yet during those times when words of praise seem hypocritical, it will help to focus on who God says He is. For instance: "You are the Creator of life, you are the Sustainer of life, you are King over all creation, you are Lord over all evil (including the evil engulfing my life), you are the strength that I lack, you are the peace that I need," and so forth. When we come to God out of obedience, the feelings will follow. Maybe immediately, maybe only after persistence and patience, but eventually the feelings of closeness will return. So will the trust.

If you're reacting as I did initially, then you're probably thinking, *I don't have time to do all this. I'll just slip in a*

[1]Bill Hybels, *Too Busy Not to Pray* (Downers Grove, Illinois: InterVarsity Press, 1988).

*prayer on my way to work or listen to a Christian radio station
or an inspirational tape.* Believe me, it's not the same. Although these are valuable supplements, they cannot replace
quality time alone with the Lord in uninterrupted quiet. I
have found that reserving time to get alone with God actually saves the time I might otherwise spend anxiously
spinning my wheels apart from His guidance.

Another significant aspect of prayer is listening. Although this is probably the most frequently forgotten or
neglected element of prayer, it is also the most important
to remember. After all, how many close friendships develop
when one person does all the talking? And even if you think
you don't have anything to say to God on a given day, He
probably has something to communicate to you.

Assuming we do want to listen to what God has to say,
how, then, does He speak to us? Of the many ways God
reveals himself, one of the most direct is through His Word.
Yet, even reading the Bible can be a painful experience for
someone recovering from sexual violence. Many well-inten-
tioned friends may direct us to passages that confuse or
even anger us as we try to find meaning in the midst of great
pain. Hopefully, the following section will help you discover
where to find comfort in the Bible.

24

Why Can't I Find Comfort
in the Bible?

"I just can't find comfort by reading the Bible."

"Well, have you read the Psalms? That book is full of comfort. I always go to the Psalms when I'm feeling down."

How many times have we heard conversations like this one? It seems whenever someone is in need of comfort, we think first of the Psalms. But when a victim of sexual violence is directed to the Psalms, this is what she may find:

> "Rescue me, O Lord, from evil men; protect me from men of violence" (Psa. 140:1, NIV).
>
> *Why didn't you rescue me, Lord? Why didn't you protect me from being attacked?*

> " 'Because he loves me,' says the Lord, 'I will rescue him; I will protect him, for he acknowledges my name' " (Psa. 91:14, NIV).
>
> *But I loved you, Lord, and I acknowledged your name. I must have done something wrong. What did I do to deserve this?*

> "For the Lord loves the just and will not forsake his faithful ones. They will be protected forever" (Psa. 37:28, NIV).

I feel so forsaken. God must not love me. I guess I wasn't faithful enough.

"No one whose hope is in you will ever be put to shame" (Psa. 25:3, NIV).

I believed in you, I trusted you, and I hoped in you. And I feel shame. I guess this promise is for everyone else, but not for me.

"The wicked lie in wait for the righteous, seeking their very lives; but the Lord will not leave them in their power or let them be condemned when brought to trial" (Psa. 37:32–33, NIV).

He got off and I'm the one condemned to live with all this mess to clean up. What about you, God? Why should I trust your promises? Where is your justice now?

Some victims may find comfort in the Psalms, especially if their assault is not the first time their faith in God's goodness has been challenged by hardship. But, like many others, I had a difficult time reading from this book following my rape, since I found so many promises of safety and protection there. I concluded that either there was something wrong with me; or God picked the ones He would love and care for and I was not one of them; or God was just not to be trusted. It wasn't until I looked at the suffering of Jesus that I was able to rebuild a relationship with God. In fact, I had to come back to Jesus (my brother) before I could come back to God (my Father).

In order to feel encouraged, a victim will first need to find Scripture that validates her feelings, such as the following:

"In the days of his flesh, Jesus offered up prayers and supplications, with loud cries and tears, to him who was able to save him from death, and he was heard for his godly fear" (Heb. 5:7).

Even Jesus cried. And He shouted out at least one of His prayers to God. He knew anguish. I guess it's okay for me to cry and shout at God in anguish, too.

"In the temple courts he found men selling cattle,

sheep and doves, and others sitting at tables exchanging money. So he made a whip out of cords, and drove all from the temple area, both sheep and cattle; he scattered the coins of the money changers and overturned their tables. To those who sold doves he said, 'Get these out of here! How dare you turn my Father's house into a market!' " (John 2:14–16, NIV).

Jesus knew anger, even outrage. He hated injustice. He must understand my anger. He must hate that I was raped.

"I have chosen you and not cast you off; fear not, for I am with you, be not dismayed, for I am your God; I will strengthen you, I will help you, I will uphold you with my victorious right hand" (Isa. 41:9b–10).

He knows I feel cast off, afraid, and dismayed. Maybe He is here for me. Maybe He will strengthen and help me after all.

"Now from the sixth hour there was darkness over all the land until the ninth hour. And about the ninth hour Jesus cried with a loud voice, 'Eli, Eli, la'ma sabach-tha'ni?' that is, 'My God, my God, why hast thou forsaken me?' " (Matt. 27:45–46).

Jesus felt forsaken by God, too. He knows what it means to feel completely alone.

"Let us fix our eyes on Jesus, the author and perfecter of our faith, who for the joy set before him endured the cross, scorning its shame, and sat down at the right hand of the throne of God. Consider him who endured such opposition from sinful men, so that you will not grow weary and lose heart" (Heb. 12:2–3, NIV).

Jesus knew shame. He scorned it. He endured incredible opposition by sinful men who hurt Him terribly. He alone can understand what I feel, and He went through all this willingly, so I won't become discouraged and lose heart. He does love me. I will focus on Him.

"The Lord is near to the brokenhearted, and saves the crushed in spirit. Many are the afflictions of the righteous; but the Lord delivers him out of them all" (Psa. 34:18–19).

If even the righteous are afflicted, brokenhearted, and crushed in spirit, then maybe there's hope for me.

"For he who is in you is greater than he who is in the world" (1 John 4:4b).

If God is more powerful than Satan, then He is certainly more powerful than the one who raped me. Together we can conquer all this damage.

Once I could see Jesus as a fellow sufferer who cried, who felt angry, forsaken, and shamed by the opposition of sinful men, I also began to see how He could know and understand every other emotion I had ever experienced. He knew what it felt like to be alone and misunderstood. He felt broken, weary, betrayed, abandoned, denied, and rejected by those closest to Him. Hanging naked on the cross, He endured humiliation, mockery, and unspeakable pain. The closer I examined the life of Jesus, the more I realized He alone could understand what I felt.

Yet as I became bonded to Jesus by suffering, there were still times when I felt anger toward God for allowing His own Son (and me) to endure so much. After all, He was God. Couldn't He have accomplished His purposes some easier way? What kind of father kills his own son?

When we are in the crisis period following sexual violence, our perspective is temporarily lost. It's like standing before a carnival mirror: the picture, both of ourselves and of God, becomes distorted. In fact, distortion is one of the biggest accomplishments Satan can claim following a rape. Recovery becomes the grueling process of sorting out the truth from the myriad of lies the Evil One would like us to go on believing.

It would have been easy for me to walk away from the Bible altogether following my rape. Many victims do, at least for a while. As it was, I found it necessary to avoid some of my favorite passages of Scripture while I looked in other places in the Bible for comfort. Having to set aside certain verses left me feeling discouraged and fearful that maybe some of the Bible was not true. But this was distortion talking.

Most victims find it difficult to understand how God could allow them to be raped in light of all His promises. Some people have even suggested I was raped so that I could write a book and minister to others. No, I do not believe that. I was raped because Roger Gray committed an act of sin, which was an offense against God. The killing of God's Son was also a transgression of the law of God. Truth shattered the glass of distortion as I discovered that although God had supreme authority over both events, He was not responsible for my rape nor for His Son's death. Satan was. When I could picture God as a compassionate Father who grieved with me and hated rape even more than I did, I could then begin the process of returning my trust to Him.

Is God weak or powerless, then, because He did not intervene? On the contrary! In time, with an expanded perspective, I came to see firsthand the truth of 1 John 4:4: "He who is in you is greater than he who is in the world." Satan may be the prince of this world (John 12:31, 14:30, 16:11), but God is King over all (1 Tim. 6:15; Psa. 103:19). He always has the final say. Sin may have stolen an inner-city ministry from me, but God brought victory through recovery and a new ministry to victims of sexual violence. If we allow Him to, God will not only "restore to you the years which the swarming locust has eaten" (Joel 2:25), but will add blessings as well.

Today if you quoted Romans 8:28 to me, "And we know that in all things God works for the good of those who love him, who have been called according to his purpose," I would say, "Amen!" But if you had referred me to that verse while I was facing the painful wounds brought on by my rape, I probably would have become angry with you and with "your God" who was allowing me to suffer so. Victims need to be given time to grieve (Eccl. 3:4).

Eventually I was able to return to my favorite passages of Scripture, including the Psalms, with a deeper, richer understanding of their message. Although it did take time and healing, I can now read the same verses that once distressed me and again find comfort and beauty in them. When I had recovered enough to stop screaming, "Why?" and began to gently ask, "Who?" . . . "Who are you, Lord?" then I was able to find both peace and a perspective that allowed me to fully return to Him. Ultimately, I was able to see that God is who He says He is, and that He does love and take care of His own.

25

Do I Need Counseling?

Many Christians believe that we should not seek counsel from anyone other than God himself. It is my belief that one of the many ways God meets our needs is through other people; people He has blessed with unique gifts, talents, and abilities. God has given us community so we can love and care for one another in a variety of ways. If I need a house, should I build it myself? If I have appendicitis, should I perform my own surgery? Likewise, in times of deep emotional, psychological, and spiritual crisis, God does not intend for us to struggle in isolation.

Upon initial contact with a victim, usually one of my first recommendations is that she begin to set up her support system. *Ideally*, she will be able to include some or, at best, all of the following: family, friends, professional counselors, clergy, and community sexual assault services. Depending on her community, other services may also be available, such as a victim/witness program provided by the courts.

Some victims immediately follow through by reaching out for help, but most find it takes tremendous courage to even begin the process of "telling others." As has been stated before, by the very nature of the crime, trust has been broken. Taking a risk by involving others in her recovery will be the victim's first step toward rebuilding trust in relationships. It is vitally important, therefore, that those she confides in display sensitivity in this area; any further violation of trust becomes intensely traumatic.

Although I am acutely aware of the difficulty involved, if I were beginning my process of recovery today, I would seek help from as many sources as possible. I would also encourage my family members to do the same, for with sexual violence there is never just one victim.

While supporting victims over the years, I have found that success in recovery is directly proportional to the amount of support and quality of counsel the victim receives. Those who do not reach out for help, but choose to stay in denial, almost always compound the problems they eventually need to resolve. These piggyback issues can be serious and always involve further loss. Those who depend on only one or two others for help will find these support people cannot (and should not be expected to) always be there for them. During the absentee times, then, the victim is left with unmet expectations, resulting in disappointment, anger, feelings of rejection and alienation, and additional negative emotions that will need to be resolved.

Normally when people ask if I recommend counseling for victims of sexual violence, they are really questioning the need for professional counseling. My hope is that if you have read this far, then you have seen enough to realize that recovery from sexual violence is a complex process. Can a victim recover without professional counseling? Many do. But I'm convinced that with good counseling the recovery process is smoother, quicker, more effective, more comprehensive, and, in the long run, less taxing on those supporting the victim. Furthermore, in some cases, especially where little or no other support is available, professional counseling may make a life-or-death difference.

How, then, does one proceed to choose a counselor? Because many victims of sexual violence may fear men in general, it can be particularly difficult to seek help from a male counselor. However, I have found that in most cases men have a high level of compassion for victims of sexual violence, as they tend to feel ashamed of the crimes others

of their gender are committing against women. Women, on
the other hand, may have more difficulty overcoming a tendency to blame the victim. Unless a female counselor can
conclude that the victim either asked for it in some way or
could have prevented the attack, she will be forced to face
the fearful realization that this horrible crime can happen
to anyone, including herself. (These are also the reasons
male jurors tend to be more sympathetic to the victim than
female jurors.) Nevertheless, unless there are exceptional
circumstances, it is best not to choose a counselor based
upon any preconceived assumptions about either sex, as
there will be variables both ways.

In the past, informed counselors in the area of sexual
violence were rare and difficult to find. I have heard more
horror stories in this regard than I care to remember. For
example, many counselors (well-educated psychologists
and psychiatrists) have erroneously equated rape with having your house broken into or recovering from a minor car
accident. Fortunately, in recent years, there has been an
upsurge of awareness on the part of such professionals.

Dr. Dan Allender, counselor, teacher, and author of *The
Wounded Heart: Hope for Adult Victims of Childhood Sexual
Abuse*, has become a pioneer in the field of sexual abuse. He
travels extensively, offering instruction to ministers, counselors, and laypeople through his seminars. Dr. Allender has
become acutely aware of the need for sexually abused clients to receive counsel that will bring about effective recovery:

> One of my counseling clients looked me in the eye
> and said, "You don't know anything about sexual
> abuse, do you?" Allender recalls.
>
> I had to tell her that in eleven years of college—
> including seminary and a five-year Ph.D. program in
> counseling psychology at Michigan State Univer-
> sity—I did not have one minute of instruction on sex-
> ual abuse.
>
> I knew some people were abused, but I never saw
> connections to other problems such as depression,
> eating disorders, and bad marriages.

Now Allender is well aware of the psychological damage sexual abuse can do. He recently calculated that twenty-six of his thirty female clients and nine of his fifteen male clients have been sexually abused.[1]

Tim Jackson, senior counselor for the Radio Bible Class biblical correspondence department, echoes Allender's statements with statistics of his own:

> I have found in my private practice that as many as 70 to 80 percent of my clients have experienced some type of sexual abuse or sexual assault in their past. Although they come to me initially with other problems such as alcoholism, drug abuse, eating disorders, depression, and marital or other relational problems.[2]

As a recovered victim in support of recovering victims, I find it encouraging that counselors are more in tune to identifying sexual assault as an underlying issue. Although instruction about rape and sexual abuse traditionally has not been included in either graduate or post-graduate formal education, counselors are becoming more sensitive to the needs of victims of these crimes. I believe this is largely due to an awakening society in general, but also to the fact that more and more recovering victims are finding a safe enough environment (both inside and outside of the counseling setting) to come forward with their stories.

Even so, finding the right counselor can be a struggle. Sometimes a victim discovers that she and her counselor are not well-suited to working together. When this occurs after a substantial investment of time and money, the victim will be more inclined to give up than to start over with someone else. To prevent this, it is wise to ask a few questions before getting started, even if a counselor comes highly recommended. A good counselor will not be bothered by this and is likely, in fact, to encourage your questions. If he or she does object, you would be wise to keep

---

[1]Dr. Dan Allender, "Recovery Possible for Victims of Sexual Abuse," *Colorado Springs Gazette Telegraph*, November 30, 1991.
[2]Tim Jackson, telephone conversation with author.

looking. Finding the right counselor may require some "shopping around," but it will be worth the effort in the long run.

The list below (in no particular order) is offered as a guide to those in search of a Christian counselor.

1. Is the counselor willing to talk about his or her view of the process of counseling?

2. What is this counselor's philosophy of counseling? Theology of life?

3. Does this counselor base his or her counsel on biblical principles? (Be careful to avoid New Age and Eastern religion philosophies.)

4. Does the counselor make such a sharp distinction between psychological and spiritual issues that he or she sees the Lord merely as useful, rather than indispensable to the process of change?

5. Does this counselor have counseling experience in the area of sexual assault (different from sexual abuse)? If not, is the counselor willing to learn from available resources?

6. Does the counselor recognize his or her own limitations in counseling, with a willingness to seek others' expertise if necessary?

7. Will the counselor make recommendations that are immoral (such as using erotic videos to resolve sexual difficulties)?

8. Do you feel cared for by the counselor? Does the counselor listen to you and accept you? (Or do you feel judged and controlled?)

9. Is the counselor's level of care appropriate? Unfortunately, some therapists abuse the power of their positions. Trust your instincts.

10. Is this person worthy of respect, and does he or she display integrity?

11. Will this counselor help you to see your worth as a person made in the image of God, or will he or she lead you into a philosophy of "self-actualization" and thus lead you astray?

12. Is this counselor replacing your relationship with God

or is he or she gently leading you back to God?[3]

Whether or not it is possible to select a counselor who meets all the desired criteria, it is important to define expectations early in the process. If a victim's only choice is to seek long-term counsel from a non-Christian counselor, then it is even more important to reach an understanding about these issues in advance. And if a non-Christian counselor is consulted, I strongly recommend that the victim also have contact with a minister or another wise Christian mentor from time to time to work through related spiritual issues and to assure that the counsel received is not in conflict with Christian values.

Also, with a non-Christian counselor it may be advisable to predetermine and establish specific boundaries. For example, when a Christian rape victim I know related an issue to something in the Bible, her counselor's response was, "You'll just have to decide for yourself whether or not that book is outdated." This woman was so upset by the comment that she called me to say she was thinking of quitting her counseling. Because I had been in close contact with her, I knew she had made tremendous progress under this counselor's care, as the counselor was extremely knowledgeable in the area of sexual assault. After talking through her feelings, the recovering victim realized that she could "agree to disagree" with her counselor on religious issues, without sacrificing the otherwise valuable help she was receiving. However, had the Bible (or faith-related issues) been mutually agreed upon as a subject best handled by others (such as a minister), the crisis could have been avoided. Once boundaries such as these have been established, both the counselee and the counselor will need to respect them.

Whether or not a victim chooses professional counseling, she is likely to need her minister's help sometime during her recovery. This role will vary, depending on the gifts of the individual pastor and the time he is able to devote to

---

[3]Most of these questions were derived from Tim Jackson, *When Help Is Needed: A Biblical View of Counseling*, Discovery Series (Grand Rapids, Michigan: Radio Bible Class, 1992).

counseling. Occasionally, a pastor with either a special heart for victims or an expertise in counseling will take a victim under his wing, playing a vital role in her recovery. However, it is unusual for a pastor to be able to do this, since, depending on the size and demands of his congregation, the minister's responsibilities may also include preaching, teaching, administration, visitation, evangelism and outreach, long-range planning, denominational obligations, social involvements, and various other commitments, all of which are added to his family responsibilities. Although it is usually unrealistic to expect frequent, long-term counsel from a pastor, it is reasonable for a victim to talk with her minister occasionally and to ask him for informed referrals if needed.

The local sexual assault center (or program) is another important resource available to those suffering from the aftermath of sexual violence. Services will vary depending on the community, but those available may include:

1. Twenty-four-hour Telephone Hotline: This is operated by trained and supervised volunteers. Although callers often expect these volunteers to have experienced sexual assault themselves, most have not. Yet, due to intensive training, these volunteers are equipped to provide vital support for anyone touched by sexual violence at any point in the recovery process (even years after the attack).

2. Hospital Victim Assistance: Trained volunteers accompany the victim and provide information as needed (usually available on a twenty-four-hour basis). They may also provide practical help, such as supplying the victim with a sweatsuit at the hospital, since clothing is usually kept as evidence.

3. Court-related Victim Assistance: Depending on the state and local community, court-related support may be provided by a separate agency such as a victim/witness assistance program provided by the county prosecutor's office. Information pertaining to legal procedures, rights of the victim, crime victims' compensation for medical bills and counseling, and other valuable information is provided

throughout the legal process. Each victim is assigned an advocate to accompany her to legal proceedings, if desired.

3. Information and Referral: Other agencies may be recommended or supplied as needed.

4. Community Education and Consultation: Volunteers and sometimes professionals are available to provide community education programs addressing such issues as rape awareness, safety and prevention, and date/acquaintance rape. Informational meetings are offered to churches, schools, and professional and civic organizations.

5. Individual and Family Therapy: Some sexual assault centers offer professional counseling, and some of these are able to offer a limited number of sessions free of charge. Those who do not offer professional counseling may offer referrals to experienced therapists in the community.

6. Therapy Groups: These are led by a therapist and are generally close-ended (meeting for a limited time with the same group). There may be a fee, and it may be based on a sliding scale.

7. Support Groups: These groups are led by a facilitator and may be open or close-ended. Because these groups are self-help in nature, some initial recovery may be advised before entering a group. (Most victims are not ready to handle hearing other people's stories right away.) Generally, no fee is charged for support groups.

8. Emergency Shelter: A short-term respite facility such as a domestic crisis center may be available for victims unable to return to their homes.

9. Specific Treatment Programs: Sexual assault centers providing professional counselors may also offer programs designed to treat specific types of sexual assault and sexual abuse. These may include programs for adult victims of childhood rape, incestuous families, adolescent victims, adults molested as children, non-familial molestation victims, and so forth.

Additional information:

- Sexual assault services normally include help for those victimized by obscene phone calls, attempted sexual assault, and/or sexual harassment.

- Most sexual assault teams include both men and women volunteers. Services are offered to both male and female victims, as well as their family members and friends who may be having difficulty coping with their loved one's assault.
- Programs like these normally adhere to strict confidentiality (if concerned, ask about their policy), with exceptions as required by child protection laws. Other exceptions surround suicide and homicide.
- Noting the overseeing organization may be important. For example, a pro-choice organization may make strong pro-choice referrals, and a program run by the police department may focus efforts on prosecution.
- Although it may be possible to request help from a Christian volunteer, sexual assault centers are generally secular in nature.

Recovery is hard work. During setbacks and times when the desire to quit is strong, the victim's support system will be essential for both encouragement and accountability. Involvement of family, friends, professional counseling, clergy, a local sexual assault program, or, hopefully, all of the above, will help to strengthen and restore the victim in recovery.

For those who choose to become (or already are) one of these support people, may God use you in powerful ways as you help to conquer the damage left by sexual violence. Though utterances of need will far outnumber expressions of gratitude, know that you are treasured for your perseverance and devotion.

———

The author wishes to thank Tim Jackson, M.A., Th.M., L.P.C., and Radio Bible Class for information provided in this section.

Also, special thanks to the YWCA Sexual Assault Center and the Kent County Victim/Witness Assistance Program, both located in Grand Rapids, Michigan, for providing updated information used in this section. Special thanks to

Patti Haist, Argie Holliman, and Susan Heartwell.

Portions taken from the *YWCA Sexual Assault Center Manual*, compiled and partially written by Patti Haist, Carla Blinkhorn, and Kay Bylenga, YWCA Sexual Assault Center, Grand Rapids, Michigan.

26

Where's the Church?

Sadly, "Where's the church?" is one of the questions posed most frequently to me by victims recovering from sexual assault. Countless victims have encountered indifference, abandonment, and outright rejection by their churches at precisely the time they most needed the love and care of fellow Christians. It has been said that Christians do more damage to Christianity than anyone else, and the damage the church has done to victims of sexual assault and abuse can be described by no other word than "shameful." Although I acknowledge this is not true of all churches, I have seen too much to portray the problem any less harshly. The experience of a young Christian woman named Chris illustrates this clearly and poignantly.[1]

Chris had already made plans the night a friend from her church called, urging her to come to her house. When Chris said she was just about to leave to go out to dinner with her parents, the friend insisted she needed her to come. So Chris changed her plans. When she arrived at her friend's house a few minutes later, she walked in on a roaring party.

While telling her friend she was not going to stay, Chris was grabbed by a young man she knew and pulled into another room, where he raped her. As soon as he was fin-

---

[1] Real name used by permission.

ished, he opened the door to a crowd of people who had been standing there the whole time, listening to Chris scream and doing nothing to help her. Later she was told she had been set up; the man had Chris's friend lure her there because he believed Chris thought she was better than he was. Raping her was his way of putting Chris in her place. Incredibly, the friend who had called Chris to the party was the rapist's girlfriend.

Following is an excerpt from the first of many letters Chris wrote to me. When I called her to ask permission to use this, she was eager for the opportunity to share her story:

> New Year's Eve, five months ago, I was raped. My life seems to be hell ever since. My circumstances were different, though. I am nineteen as you were, but I knew my rapist. Although I never liked him, he went to my church. Also, like you, I've found out that our laws do not protect the innocent. They protect the rapists and allow them not to be punished.
>
> My whole life has completely changed. My church chose to support him and not me, and because I was a choir director, church pianist, and assistant youth director, I am not able to understand why he seems to have come out the winner and I, the loser. I am writing because I am hoping you can give me some answers I need so desperately. God has always been the center of my life, and I've been raised in a Christian home with God as our family foundation. But since New Year's Eve, I am so angry with God. Church is not a major part of my life any longer.
>
> I want answers. I want to know why. Why did God let me be raped? What did I do to deserve this awful pain and hurt I feel? Sometimes I wish the rapist would have killed me, because I hurt so deeply now. I can't date. I'm scared. I wonder if I ever will feel complete and able to love a man. I feel like screaming when I think about anyone being close to me. I'm so afraid it won't ever end.
>
> I wish so bad I could completely forget, but it's like it haunts me. I have nightmares. I've lost thirty-

three pounds. My life feels so empty and confused.
Never in my life have I felt so much hurt, so much
hate! I want to hate God. I hate the rapist, and I'm
not sure who I am anymore. He created a gap inside
of me and I'm lost.

When Chris sent this letter, she was searching for a
Christian who would offer her hope. What she needed more
than anything else was a safe place to recover. Fortunately,
Chris eventually found healing for the broken places in her
life. In fact, before she graduated from college, she started
a rape crisis center on her campus for those who had suffered as she had.

Although she did find supportive Christians elsewhere
during her recovery, Chris's support system did not include
her own church. Instead, she was asked irrelevant and hurtful questions by fellow members, like, "What were you doing there?" and "Why did you go to the party?" She could
only respond by saying she didn't know there was a party.
Because her church chose to add blame and accusation to
her trauma, Chris and her family found it necessary to
leave, after fourteen years of active membership there.

Incredibly, after three years of attending another
church, they decided to return. And it was there, in front of
this same congregation, during a Wednesday evening worship service, that Chris spoke about how God had helped
her to forgive her rapist (whose family still attended there).
It was also in this church that she married a wonderful
Christian man.

In portions from some of her later letters Chris speaks
about God and His healing in her life:

It was through the pain and hell of the rape that
I found His love, felt His arms, and saw Him face-to-
face. You do heal, it does mesh with all areas of your
life, and you're better than before. I am better in so
many ways.

There is healing and peace, there is laughter and
joy, but because I was raped doesn't mean hard times
and heartache leave me alone. But I have come

through a dark, deep valley and saw light. And that alone is my strength and hope, that with the Lord and good special friends, no valley is too deep or too dark!

Chris recovered in spite of her church. What a sad statement. Yet, both victims and victim advocates know that Chris's story of abandonment by her church is repeated again and again. Author Candace Walters speaks to this when she writes about her experience as a rape crisis counselor in the article, "The Wounds of Rape":

What happens when a rape victim does seek solace from her church community? Unfortunately, her pain may intensify. I have talked with dozens of victims who felt more deeply injured by the attitudes of their congregation than by the assault itself. Elizabeth was asked to stop teaching Sunday school after she was sexually attacked by a neighbor, because she was no longer a "good role model" for children. Diane was assaulted by a customer at her place of employment and then blamed by her church elders, who felt women should not work outside the home.

Sarah endured years of abuse from her husband, because her pastor told her there is no such thing as marital rape. Kelly was date raped at gunpoint by a police-academy recruit who appeared to be an exemplary young man at church. The pastor and board urged her not to press charges since it would embarrass both prominent families, and besides, it was "her word against his."[2]

Because of attitudes like this, an even worse tragedy is taking place in our churches. Countless victims are suffering within our church walls—*in silence.* Because they rightfully sense they would be blamed, misunderstood, or judged, many victims are simply choosing not to tell. As a result, they are left isolated and alone in their time of greatest need. I believe sexual assault is one of the most powerful

---

[2]Candace Walters with Beth Spring, "The Wounds of Rape," *Christianity Today,* September 14, 1992. Used by permission of author.

ways Satan is damaging the church today. And he's doing it silently, without people knowing.

One of the most painful expressions I ever have to hear is, "That's just not a problem in our church." Unfortunately, many people believe this—and it's just not true. Almost all of the sexual assault victims who have contacted me, seeking support, have been Christians. In fact, if my own congregation only knew all the people in our church who have shared their stories with me in confidence, they would be shocked, not only by the numbers, but by the fact that these are all people they know. Even victims themselves have no idea how many others have suffered as they have.

Candace Walters also addresses this attitude in her article:

> "That's not a problem in our church." I hear this often, even as women active in their denominations or congregations are contacting me, crying for help. These victims face a sad predicament when it comes to their churches. Many pastors say rape victims seek counsel from them rarely, if ever. But this does not mean women in their churches are unaffected; it means few victims ask for help. The victim may sense, often correctly, that the church would respond inappropriately.[3]

Just who is the victim of sexual violence? To the people in her congregation, she does not look anything like the typical magazine article's shadowy, mysterious, tear-streaked face artistically depicted behind a shattered window. She may be the fifty-six-year-old woman who leads the choir into the sanctuary every Sunday, the one who always stands in the front row of the soprano section. She may be the young mother laughing with a friend in the church parking lot after the service. Perhaps she is the energetic teenager who helps with the four- and five-year-old Sunday school class, the same one who is always there to help wash cars at the youth group fund-raisers. The victim may also be the man greeting people with a smile as he

---

[3]Ibid.

hands out bulletins near the back of the church. He might even be the seven-year-old boy who, dressed like a shepherd, forgets his line at the Christmas program. Although these are all hypothetical examples, any rape crisis team will tell you this is an accurate representation of those being victimized today.

The FBI estimates that one in three females and one in seven males will be victimized by sexual assault sometime in their lifetime. Not only are Christians not immune, but many believe they are more vulnerable to attack because of faulty attitudes such as: "We will be protected from rape if we pray for protection, if we're living a godly life, and/or if we don't bring evil upon ourselves by sinning." I prayed daily for God to protect me. Some of the most godly people I know became victims of rape, including pastors' wives. And as has already been stated more than once in this book, people are raped because the rapist sins, not the victim.

As Christians, we are also more vulnerable to attack because of our lack of desire to deal with these issues within the church setting. When pastors are afraid to say the word "rape" from the pulpit, congregations are given permission to keep it in the closet. When we look the other way with our attitudes, we not only neglect the victim; we also allow the rapist to keep on raping, sometimes within the church. To borrow a saying from the sixties, "If you are not part of the solution, you are part of the problem."

Again, I quote Candace Walters:

> For ten years, I have worked as a rape crisis counselor and a community education specialist on sexual violence. Consistently, the church's lack of interest has been one of the most frustrating and saddening aspects of my work. The rape crisis center where I volunteer, which serves a city of more than one million people, receives hundreds of requests each year for speakers on rape education and prevention. These requests come from businesses, schools, philanthropic groups, political organiza-

tions, and even men's clubs, but hardly ever from churches.[4]

Many churches recognize that there is a problem, but choose not to deal with it because they don't feel equipped to handle it. Some pastors actually fear the day someone in their church will come to them for help. Those who have no qualms about ministering to individual victims may be quite anxious about opening a congregation-wide Pandora's box. They are not only afraid of finding out *how many* victims there are, but also *who* they are.

As an additional barrier, many ministers fear that counseling victims will lead to the discovery of rapists within their own congregations. How, then, do they handle these offenders? Issues include: How do they decide who needs to be told versus when to honor confidentiality? Will confronting an assailant within the church damage or destroy unity? (Remember, the perpetrator of the crime is the one responsible for the damage.) How does the church approach discipline when the offender is a member or perhaps even a leader in the church? These are all legitimate concerns, but a crime is a crime. (If the assailant was a murderer rather than a rapist, would the approach be different?) Besides, what is the alternative? If we look the other way, who will become the next victim?[5]

If the church's attitude is, "We can't solve it, so we can't help," then where will it stop? In a recent sermon, one of my pastors stated that God does not hear the word "can't." When we say the word "can't," what God hears is "won't."

I believe the place to begin dealing with the whole issue of sexual assault within the church is with ministry to victims.

When I spoke with Chris about using her story for this section of the book, she expressed some of her thoughts about the church; I believe she speaks for many victims:

> You know, it seems strange to realize that the

---

[4]Ibid.
[5]Material in this section is adapted from the author's conversation with Rev. Michael Bos of Sunshine Church, Grand Rapids, Michigan.

same people who were there for us at our wedding, the ones who supported us when my mother died, are the same people who hurt us so at the time of my rape. I think they hurt us out of ignorance. Churches need to know that it's OK if they're not equipped to solve the victim's problems for her. They need to know that nobody can give her answers, that she has to find them for herself. But, if they could just say to us, "We may not have answers and we may not understand, but we're going to be here for you." All they have to be is compassionate and caring.

A victim of sexual violence appreciates cards, notes of encouragement, prayers, flowers, plates of cookies, and a listening ear just as much as the grieving widow does. A caring friend can go to the bookstore and find a book on sexual assault, as, initially, a victim may feel too overwhelmed to do this for herself. Friends can donate books to their church libraries on sexual assault and abuse, fear, forgiveness, prayer, and other related subjects.

One or two church members can arrange for community specialists to speak in their church about sexual violence, extending special invitations to pastors and other church leaders to attend. There is no reason pastors cannot become informed at the same time as their parishioners. Teenagers may also attend if a special effort is made to include them. A series could be planned to include representatives from the local rape crisis center, the police, the court's victim/witness program, and the medical and counseling fields. If the church is small, this could be planned jointly with another church in the community.

Just because these speakers or groups are not established by the Christian community does not mean we cannot learn from them. Frankly, I don't believe God would object to a police officer instructing church members about the dangers of crime in the community, even if the officer's language may be a little rough around the edges. No doubt God is more offended by the lack of care our churches display while, one after the other, His sheep are being physically, emotionally, psychologically, and spiritually damaged by sexual violence.

In the practical sense, it is wise for churches to pay attention to whether or not they are "victim friendly." For instance, I once visited a church where the congregation was instructed to turn to the person next to them and extend a warm, welcoming hug. A moment like this can be devastating for a recovering victim of sexual assault, especially if she is sitting next to someone she has never met. Intimate bodily contact should always be the choice of both individuals, never forced by someone else in authority. This is true for children as well as adults. There are many ways a church can promote friendliness without manipulating the expression of it.

As a note to pastors, during my own recovery one of the most painful words for me to hear in church was "angels." (It's amazing how many hymns refer to angels, let alone sermons.) As a recovering victim I wondered—as many will—where God's angels were while I was being assaulted. I always appreciated hearing sermons that were sensitively preached when dealing with the concept of angels and/or God's protection.

Other ways to become "victim friendly" may include: installing security devices on buildings, providing well-lighted parking lots, promoting an atmosphere where gossip is curtailed and confidences are kept, carefully screening laypeople for authority positions, and taking a proactive stand against alcohol abuse and pornography.

On the bright side, some churches have not only become "victim friendly," but have also found specific ways to assist victims in the recovery process. Churches organizing support groups have received so many responses that victims are often placed on waiting lists before being assigned a group. A word of caution, however: it is important to have a trained resource person as a consultant, and group leaders need to be aware of their own limitations, since support groups are meant to supplement professional counseling, not replace it. Often these groups meet in homes, announcing their meetings only to those involved to provide anonymity for any who desire it.

Some say churches will not become supportive until victims come forward, but most victims will not come forward until churches become supportive. Unless we intend to sit back and let evil win, the cycle must be broken, and it will take courage on the part of both churches and victims to accomplish this. Every church can do something to help. Getting started is the key. Once churches begin to listen without condemnation to the cries of recovering victims, caring for them in tangible ways will become a natural response.

God first looks for the heart, and then, by the extension of His all-sufficient hand, He provides the way. May we all look to Him for wisdom, guidance, and clear direction as we seek to love Him more through ministry to His hurting people. And may victims like Chris and her family never again have to leave their churches to find the love of God and His healing in their lives.

27

What About Abortion in the Case of Rape?

Until recent years, I was not sure what I thought about abortion in the case of rape and incest. Since I did not become pregnant as a result of my rape, it never became an issue for me personally. Also, in fifteen years of supporting rape victims, including one year on my local rape crisis team, I have never been in a position to offer counsel to a victim impregnated by her rapist. Such cases are known to be rare.

Over the years I did occasionally wonder what I might have done if a pregnancy had resulted from my rape. Bob and I had only been dating for four months at the time I was attacked, and abortion was not legal in Illinois in 1969 (except for the preservation of the life of the mother). I had only completed one year of my college education, and at that time I had plans to become a teacher. It's probably unfair to speculate about what I would have done, since no one can say for sure unless they are actually in the situation. I can only say that my life would have been much different. It certainly could have been called an unwanted pregnancy, as it would have disrupted all the plans I had for my life, and I would have been carrying the child of a rapist. Both harsh realities.

I had always considered myself to be primarily pro-life, but in the case of rape and incest, I wondered if maybe there was reason to make an exception. Then in November 1988, the citizens of Michigan were asked to vote on a proposal to end tax-funded abortions in our state, even in the case of rape and incest, and I had to decide once and for all where I stood on the issue. As I studied both sides, one thought kept coming back to me: *but this is a life.* Still, it seemed heartless to suggest that anyone dealing with a rape should also be expected to handle a pregnancy, especially if she could legally choose otherwise. After all, I had nearly committed suicide, and I wasn't even pregnant. What right did I have to tell someone else she should add an unwanted pregnancy to the trauma of her rape?

Asking all the hard questions, I attended both pro-life and pro-choice community talks. I delved into books, articles, and clinical studies, gathering facts and statistics from both sides. Yet no matter what the reasoning or argument on either side, I still kept coming back to one fact: *this is a life.* Do we have a right to end a life? Even if the circumstances appear unbearable?

During this time, I thought about all the difficulties a victim has to face following a rape. As I reflected on my own experience and the experiences of others I had supported, it occurred to me that if we really wanted to ease a victim's recovery, then ending the life of the rapist would make more sense than ending the life of the unborn child. Over the years, many victims had expressed their thoughts to me about killing the men who had raped them. If we allowed this, then a victim would never have to live in fear of her rapist again, and what trauma that would save! Of course, I do not suggest we actually do this; neither did these victims. Yet, how irrational it is that we have laws to protect the life of a rapist, but none to protect the life of his innocent child.

As the time to vote approached, the debate heated up. And it was then that I found myself becoming angry with the pro-choice side. They zeroed in on the rape and incest issue, declaring that should a poor victim become pregnant as a result of such sexual assault, no one could possibly expect her to carry that life to term. Their tactics clearly were to divert attention away from the unborn life and focus on the hardship of the mother.

What made me even angrier was the underlying pro-choice message: The rape victim is in a shameful state and so is the life she is carrying, so surely she must want to dispose of it. They attached shame and disgrace to both the victim and the child, when in reality the shame and disgrace belong exclusively to the rapist. In our throwaway society, they found it more expedient to terminate the life that makes people uncomfortable than to display truthful attitudes toward victims and offer their support.

In reality, then, despite all their sympathetic rhetoric, these pro-choice factions did not have the best interest of rape and incest victims in mind. They were using the victims' plight to promote their own pro-choice agenda. Under the guise of compassion, they suggested we add one more victim to the crime, this time by terminating the life of a developing unborn child. Yet, one had to ask: Why should that child suffer the death penalty for the crime of the father?

Furthermore, I also came to realize that promoting abortion in the case of incest means the perpetrator is given the freedom to continue his criminal behavior, for abortion destroys the evidence. Abortion does not relieve the problem of incest; it only hides it. Again the pro-choice agenda usurped the best interest of the victim.

After studying both sides of the issue, I concluded that no matter how seemingly unbearable the circumstances, ending a life is not a compassionate answer.

For those who support the right to choose, the following food for thought is an appeal to their moral conscience:

> Many people have heard the line, "I'm personally opposed to abortion, but I support the right to choose." Turn the argument on its head: How much sense does it make to say, "I'm personally opposed to rape, but I support the right to choose"? Clearly, our society does not permit choice without consideration

of the choices made. Generally, the exercise of one person's rights ends when those of another person are threatened. My right to swing my fist ends at the tip of your nose; similarly, a woman's right to choose what she does to her body ought to end when that choice kills her dependent, yet distinct, unborn child.[1]

As I found myself agreeing with the Right to Life position in these cases, however, I did wonder: Have I become hardened to the plight of the pregnant victim? This was all still so theoretical.

Then, about a year later, I met Lee Ezell. When I discovered Lee was to speak at Praise Gathering in Indianapolis, I was anxious to hear her, since I had read her book, *The Missing Piece*, in which she tells how she became pregnant in 1963 as a result of rape. Facing the situation alone at the age of eighteen, she met a modern-day Good Samaritan family who offered her their home and their love and support. When her baby was born, Lee bravely and lovingly gave her up for adoption. More than twenty years later, she and her child conceived in rape, Julie Makimaa, were reunited. Lee's story presents a powerful message of God's faithfulness and the way He works His purposes in our lives.[2]

At the end of Lee's talk that day in Indianapolis, she surprised us all by introducing Julie. Afterward, I met both of them, and Julie and I corresponded for some time. Our paths have crossed a couple of times since then, and each time I see Julie, I am captivated by a singular thought: By the message our society sends in its laws, this beautiful, vibrant young lady ought not to exist. What is even more sobering is to hear Julie talk about her husband, and to see pictures of her two children. Anyone who wonders whether

---

[1]"Dealing with the Hard Questions: A Few Suggestions," prepared by the Right to Life of Michigan Legislative Office, Right to Life of Michigan Education Office, 2340 Porter St., S.W., P.O. Box 901, Grand Rapids, Michigan 49509–0901.

[2]Lee Ezell, *The Missing Piece* (Ann Arbor, Michigan: Servant Publications, 1992).

criminal behavior is hereditary, whether the child of a rapist will be evil or whether these children will suffer terrible psychological problems, has only to look into Julie's eyes and hear her speak. Any such notion is quickly shattered. It is also clear from all those involved, especially Julie's parents who raised her, that an unwanted pregnancy does not mean an unwanted child.

In addition to her legislative lobbying efforts, Julie has formed an organization called Fortress International, dedicated to women who become pregnant as a result of rape or incest, as well as to children conceived in rape.[3] To date, Julie has worked with 350 women who became pregnant through rape or incest. Of those who carried their baby to term, none has ever told her they regret their decision. But the women who had abortions in these circumstances have struggled hard with the knowledge that they chose to take the life of their child.

From all that I have seen and read, I have concluded that recovering from an abortion in these instances is often more difficult than recovering from the rape itself. This only makes sense. In a rape, the woman is the victim; but in an abortion, she is the aggressor.

As I became more involved in pro-life activities, I noticed a hardening of my own heart toward those who had chosen abortion. Hoping to soften my view and to learn more about the abortion experience, I decided to attend a weekend conference presented by Open ARMs, a ministry to those suffering after abortion.[4] It was sobering to witness the deep remorse and overwhelming guilt that many displayed. Hearing stories of horrible deception and misinformation, I began to view many of these women as victims of the abortion industry.

To my knowledge, none of these women had been raped. But as I listened to their stories, I heard them expressing the same trauma a rape victim suffers during her recovery: grief, shame, loneliness, low self-worth, depression, sad-

---

[3]Fortress International, P.O. Box 642, Lake City, Florida 32056.
[4]Open ARMs (Abortion Related Ministries), National Office, P.O. Box 1056, Columbia, Missouri 65205.

ness, numbness, denial, anger/rage, sexual problems, night-mares, and suicidal urges. Added to this list is the inability to forgive oneself. Although through this ministry and others like it many learn to take responsibility for their choice and eventually find healing, I came away from the weekend concluding that abortion only adds trauma to trauma in the case of rape or incest. The victim trades the relief of a short-term solution for the grief of a long-term problem.

No, suggesting abortion in the case of rape and incest is not the compassionate answer. Providing the support necessary for the woman to carry the developing life to term is. Besides, as Christians, if we choose otherwise, are we not saying, "God, you are just not big enough to handle this one"?

Following is an excerpt from an article appearing in *Concerned Women in America,* written by one of their staff members. Impregnated by her rapist, this young woman faced numerous difficulties: harassment from a co-worker who pressured her to have an abortion, withdrawal of professional support from her (now former) employer, a doctor who would have preferred the financial security of an abortion patient, and an insurance company who seemed reluctant to honor her policy. Although her immediate family was supportive, her extended family disagreed with her course of action. All of these people sent her a message of defeat: *You do not have a choice; you should have an abortion.* In spite of all the obstacles, this young woman offers a powerful message of her own, validating the notion that giving birth to life may be the single most positive thing a victim can do about her rape.

I was fully cognizant of all the factors involved in becoming a single mom. I chose to have my baby. And I chose to keep her. My choice of life was founded on certain laws of God which I believe are inviolable no matter what the mitigating circumstances might be.

I suppose it could have been possible to disobey God for the sake of my career, my state of mind, or my convenience. But the consequences of that, such as living with the knowledge that I'd killed my baby and the grief such a murder would bring to the Holy Spirit, were weighty enough to convince me that there was really no choice as long as I was going to be accountable to God. . . .

Despite the time and energy so many put into influencing me to circumvent God's plans and the blessings wrought by His healing hand, I find myself now joyfully trying to keep up with a blue-eyed, curly-headed, abundantly healthy little girl who loves apples, music, her teddy bear, and her Uncle Ben. The question whether I resented (or still resent) carrying the seed of an angry, insensitive, selfish man who abused my personal rights and violated my understanding of loving relationships is out of context. No one asks me that question now, because they have seen the fruit of that seed. I feel as though God reached into my life with a blessing, with the miracle of new life. I know the love of God because He has given me a beautiful gift. In this and in returning His care, I found healing. Scriptural study, prayer, fellowship, and worship were the balms He used to heal my wounds.

An abortion would have brought none of this.[5]

The author wishes to thank Right to Life of Michigan for providing information used in this section, with special thanks to Barb Listing.

---

[5]"Divine Grace: The Story of a Rape Victim Who Chose Life," *Concerned Women in America*, April 1990. (The author chooses to remain anonymous because of possible contact by her attacker.)

28

Why Should I Forgive?

"Why should I forgive my rapist? He doesn't deserve it."
Even Christian victims feel this way. But somehow we know
we are supposed to forgive the people who hurt us.

As God fashioned recovery in my life, He also accomplished forgiveness in my heart for the man who had raped
me. Yet it has always been difficult for me to express how
this happened. I can point to no singular, dramatic moment
when I forgave Roger Gray. Although I had expressed forgiveness for him in prayer many times, none of these moments were so remarkable that I can even remember when
they occurred. Forgiveness was a process; it was accomplished over time. This has always bothered me somewhat,
since I never know quite what to say to those who ask how
I forgave him. Through another crisis in my life, however,
when once again forgiveness was required, God finally dispelled some of the mystery.

Several years ago I suffered severe abdominal pain, so
severe that my gynecologist at first suspected a ruptured
ovarian cyst. But neither an ultrasound nor laparoscopic
surgery revealed any sign of a cyst. When I brought up my
history of endometriosis to three different doctors, each one
stated that because I had undergone a hysterectomy two
years before that time, they were ruling out endometriosis.
After numerous procedures and tests, my doctors diagnosed

the problem as irritable bowel syndrome, a condition brought on by stress.

For months I accepted their diagnosis, even though it did not make sense to me. Sometimes when I was under a lot of stress, the pain was not worse; and during less stressful times, it was often unbearable. In spite of this and the fact that I did not display other symptoms common to irritable bowel syndrome, the doctors stood firm with their diagnosis. After months of following their dietetic program and finding no relief, I began to search for answers myself. One day, while paging through medical books in the library, I became so weak that I passed out. Even though the prescribed doses of painkillers had not begun to touch my pain, the medication had been too strong for my system to handle.

Little by little I gave up my usual activities, until I eventually became bedridden from both the pain and the heavy doses of medication. About a year after all this began, on a night neither of us will forget, Bob drove me to the hospital emergency room. I was writhing in pain. After a hypodermic of some sort, which I was told would wear off a couple of hours later, they released me.

I will never forget the look on Bob's face as he uttered, "They're sending you home?" After speaking with my doctor on the phone, the medical personnel in attendance told me there was nothing more they could do for me, since my tests had shown nothing unusual. But apparently I had finally gotten this doctor's attention, because after that night he referred me to yet another specialist.

Less than two days after my appointment with him, this specialist, recognizing the severity of my illness, performed major exploratory surgery. He suspected endometriosis and found it, removing both ovaries. Eight days later, addicted to the pain medication I had taken for a year and weighing ninety-six pounds, I left the hospital.

Later I was told by a gynecologist from Mayo Clinic in Rochester, Minnesota, that it is not uncommon for endometriosis to show up following a hysterectomy. He did not dispute my conclusion that my three original doctors should have suspected it.

I was furious. I had lost a year of my life, and the cost to our family could never be grasped, let alone repaid. Not only did none of the three doctors ever admit to their misdiagnosis, but one insisted that the surgeon who found the endometriosis must have been wrong. Even though this doctor knew I was no longer in pain, and even though the pathology report had confirmed endometriosis, he still would not admit his diagnosis had been wrong.

Some time later I made the mistake of going to another doctor associated with one of the three for a totally unrelated problem. I needed medical help for back pain brought on by some vigorous walking I had done. This doctor offered nothing, except to suggest that counseling might help me.

The anger within me grew. Some days I tried to find excuses for each of the doctors, rationalizing that endometriosis was known to be difficult to diagnose. I tried to make myself believe everything was fine now. Sometimes this worked. Then, without warning, anger would spew out of me. Eventually I realized that, regardless of my feelings, I was not going to hear the words "I'm sorry" from any of them, and I would have to learn to live with that.

After a few visits with a counselor and the passing of some time, I came to recognize that my anger was compounding the damage that had already been done to our family. Furthermore, I was at risk of becoming a bitter person. I decided I needed to forgive these doctors, not because they deserved to be forgiven, and not because I felt like it, but for myself—for my own health and for the well-being of our family. Another motivation was the fact that Communion services had become a problem for me. My harbored resentments were interfering with my relationship with God, because forgiveness was something He expected.

During that time, it occurred to me that I was having a harder time forgiving these doctors than I'd had forgiving the man who had raped me. But why? Certainly the devastation had been greater following my rape. After some reflection, I figured it out.

I had lived in the inner city for five weeks before Roger Gray raped me. I had seen the crowded, sparsely furnished, run-down apartments and row houses. I had watched as people paid twenty-five cents for a secondhand shirt to wear to church, and a dollar for a kitchen chair. I had seen hopelessness in the eyes of alcoholic parents, and fear in the faces of their neglected children. I had witnessed poor health conditions and insufficient wages for hard factory jobs that anyone from my neighborhood would have quit in a week. Yet these people clung to their jobs just to pay the rent and put food on the table.

Recalling all this, I had concluded that if I had been forced to grow up in these conditions, I might not have turned out any different than the man who had raped me. This was not to make excuses for him; many people did survive conditions like these without becoming criminals. I still held him responsible for what he had done to me. But I had been able to equate myself with him as a sinner before God.

In the case of my doctors, however, I thought differently. *They should have known better,* I thought. I could not equate myself with them. In fact, I felt slightly superior. After all, if I were a doctor, I would not practice medicine the way they did. I would have listened to my patient, rather than insisting my diagnosis could not be wrong. Besides, forgiving them would not be fair. I'd had to go through all that pain. Why should I just let them off the hook? I was the one who had been hurt, so why should I go out of my way to do anything for them? They hadn't even had the common decency to say, "We're sorry. We were wrong." Holding on to my anger gave me a sense of power over them, a power I did not want to relinquish. Yet I knew I had to let it go.

Some of the passages I had studied in Bible Study Fellowship that year were fresh in my mind:

Mark 11:25: And when you stand praying, if you hold anything against anyone, forgive him, so that your Father in heaven may forgive you your sins (NIV).

Matthew 6:12–15: Forgive us our debts, as we also have forgiven our debtors. And lead us not into temptation, but deliver us from the evil one. For if you forgive men when they sin against you, your heavenly Father will also forgive you. But if you do not forgive men their sins, your Father will not forgive your sins (NIV).[1]

Luke 6:37: Do not judge and you will not be judged. Do not condemn, and you will not be condemned. Forgive, and you will be forgiven (NIV).

James 2:12–13: Speak and act as those who are going to be judged by the law that gives freedom, because judgment without mercy will be shown to anyone who has not been merciful. Mercy triumphs over judgment! (NIV).

A strong message. Not to forgive those doctors was to disobey God. It was that simple. But how was I supposed to do that when I didn't *feel* at all forgiving toward them? I went back to God's Word:

Ephesians 4:31–32: Get rid of all bitterness, rage and anger, brawling and slander, along with every form of malice. Be kind and compassionate to one another, forgiving each other, just as in Christ God forgave you (NIV).

Colossians 3:13: Bear with each other and forgive whatever grievances you may have against one another. Forgive as the Lord forgave you (NIV).

Romans 3:23: For all have sinned and fall short of the glory of God, and are justified freely by his grace through the redemption that came by Christ Jesus (NIV).

Even though I was reminded by these verses that, through His Son, God had forgiven me for my sins, I still felt slightly better than the doctors I was supposed to be forgiving. I decided to go to God in obedience and trust Him to accomplish the work of forgiveness. It was during this

---

[1] I do not believe these verses raise a salvation issue. Salvation is a gift. We cannot earn it or lose it based upon our own performance. This simply means when we fail to forgive another, we cannot *claim* forgiveness for ourselves.

time alone with God that everything changed.

Taking a piece of paper, I drew a vertical line down the middle of the page. On the top of the left side I wrote, "Damage Done." Underneath this heading I wrote the names of the doctors, leaving space below each one. Then, under each name, I listed the specific things they had done that had caused me pain. Just writing down the damage caused anger and bitterness to resurface. Yet, just as I had given my fear over to God many times before, I knew I had to do the same with these emotions. God had commanded me to do so.

On the top of the right side of the paper I wrote, "Times I've Committed the Same Sin." First on my list of damages was, "He didn't listen to me." As an act of obedience, I prayed, "Lord, I give You my anger." Then I prayed, "Lord, show me a time when I committed this same sin." After a few minutes of silence, I was reminded of a time when I had not listened to my son, causing him pain. As I made a note of it on the right side of the page, I asked God to forgive me for the hurt I had caused. Then I obediently said the words, "I forgive him, too," even though the consequences of the doctor's action seemed far greater than the consequences of mine.

I moved to the next one. It read, "He insisted he was right when he wasn't." Again, after first relinquishing my right to hold on to my anger, I prayed, "Lord, show me a time when I committed this same sin." After a few minutes, I remembered a time I had hurt another person by insisting I was right, when later it turned out I had been wrong. Again, I asked God to forgive me; then I forgave my doctors. Likewise, where they had misjudged me, I had also misjudged others. Where they had not taken responsibility for their mistakes, I had done the same. As I progressed down the list, there were moments when I almost dared God to come up with a time I had committed the same sin. With persistence, patience, and the power of the Holy Spirit, I was reminded over and over of specific times I had hurt others by my attitudes and actions, sometimes going as far back as my childhood.

Although the level of the consequences did not always match, the sin was the same. As the Spirit convicted me of my own sinfulness, I came to realize that I, too, was undeserving of forgiveness. Many times, as memories washed over me, I broke down and cried. God was teaching me a powerful lesson. As I asked for and humbly received His forgiveness, I was enabled to forgive those who had hurt me. Even more, the fact that Jesus had willingly taken upon himself not only my sins, but the sins of the whole world, became real to me in a new, awesome, and unfathomable way. Jesus had suffered death on the cross for every sinner, which included me and my doctors, the criminal hanging on the cross next to Him, and every rapist and murderer who ever lived. For all time.

Can a rapist be forgiven by the same process I used to forgive my doctors? I believe by breaking down the damage and trusting God to accomplish the work, the answer is "yes." The list of damages might read something like this:

1. He did not listen when I said no.
2. He made me feel ashamed.
3. He took control of me.
4. He humiliated me.
5. He lied about what happened.
6. He violated my rights.
7. He made me fearful.
8. He damaged my feelings of self-worth.
9. He never apologized for hurting me.
10. He damaged relationships that are important to me.

I do not believe it's necessary to list every bit of damage, which would be an impossible task anyway. But spending time alone with God working through the process is vitally important, because it is here that the burden of our anger is lifted. I should add, though, that it is possible to have forgiven someone and still have anger. In some cases, new damage in need of processing may surface later. Other times, even though there has already been forgiveness, it may be necessary to reread the list as a reminder that forgiveness has been accomplished. I had to do this with my list more than once.

Forgiving does not mean we forget. Neither does it mean we excuse. We still hold rapists accountable and take them to court. But when we have forgiven the person who has hurt us, we no longer harbor malice in our hearts. I was assured that I had truly forgiven my rapist the first time I found myself praying for him. I prayed for his salvation, that he would seek and find forgiveness, and that God would restore his life from the pit. I had come to realize that even though God is angry about rape and hates what Roger Gray did, He extends His offer of redemptive love to him as well.

However, even though I have forgiven my rapist, I still have no reason to trust my physical safety to him. While I sometimes wonder whatever became of him, I have no intention of contacting him. Nor do I plan to return to any of those four doctors for medical care. These decisions are not born of anger or fear, but simply seem wise considering the circumstances as they stand today.

Both these experiences taught me that God truly has our best interest in mind when He writes His law upon our hearts. When we equate ourselves with other undeserving sinners and seek forgiveness for our sins, then we are able to forgive. And it is only when we forgive that we find freedom from anger, hate, and bitterness. Sometimes we need to exercise a deliberate act of humble obedience, such as I found necessary to forgive my doctors. Other times, perhaps without any dramatic or involved effort on our part, we will forgive the offender, as was the case with forgiving my rapist. Either way, forgiveness is a process—a process that is accomplished after enough of the anger has been forfeited and at least some healing has taken place. It should not be expected to happen too soon.

Although we are the ones who must choose to forgive, forgiveness is accomplished by God himself, in us, and through His Son. Of all His gifts, this is by far the greatest. Beyond measure. For it is through forgiveness that we find peace.

There is a greater love,
   that transcends the powers of men.
There is a greater love,
   this world can't comprehend.
A love that completes,
   a love that forgives . . .
There is a greater love,
   that can overcome all wrong.
There is a greater love,
   that's as wide as it is long.
It looks o'er the past,
   and reaches within,
There is a greater love . . .
   than even the greatest sin.[2]

I wish I could close with this triumphant declaration of victory, but I would be leading the reader astray to do so. Because I have forgiven, I am essentially at peace with myself and with God. But this is not a perfect peace. For although forgiveness has freed me from the tyranny of anger, bitterness, and malice, I am not yet free from the quiet longings of my heart. Evil cannot be completely conquered and brokenness cannot be fully restored until there is repentance on the part of my offenders. For this I continue to hope and pray, both for their sake and for mine.

———

The author gratefully acknowledges Jim Fongers, M.S.W., C.S.W., for his study of forgiveness, which contributed to the writing of this section.

———

[2]"Greater Love," from the album "Choice of a Lifetime," by Charles Billingsley. Music by Brandon Banks, words by Charles Billingsley, arranged by Marc Phillips. Copyright 1992 by Crest Music, P.O. Box 130903, Birmingham, Alabama 35213. Used by permission.

Appendix

Facts, Statistics, and Further Information

- One in three females and one in seven males will be sexually assaulted in his or her lifetime. (This includes child sexual abuse.)
- For every rape reported, the FBI estimates that ten are not. Rape remains the most underreported crime in America.
- Rapists rarely rape only once. In one study it was discovered that 126 rapists committed a total of 907 rapes involving 882 different victims. The average number of different victims was seven.[1] In sexual molestation cases, the number can be as high as fifty or more victims per one offender.
- Approximately 60% to 80% of all sexual assaults are committed by someone known to the victim. (This does not change the fact that rape is a crime.)
- Fifty percent of the offenders in rapes of females under the age of eighteen are their boyfriends.

[1]Abel, G., Becker, J., Mittelman, M., Cunningham-Rathner, J., Rouleau, J., and Murphy, W., "Self-Reported Sex Crimes of Nonincarcerated Paraphiliacs," *Journal of Interpersonal Violence*, 2 (1), 3–25, 1987, as reported in "Rape in America: A Report to the Nation."

- Most rapes (approximately 70%) are planned.
- Rapists engage in a selection process, often eliminating some women until they find a suitable victim. (Becoming a victim relates to vulnerability, not a person's dress or "provocative" manner.)
- Most rape offenders are either married or actively involved in consenting sexual relations with others.
- Over 90% of all sexual assaults involve persons of the same race.
- Although victims of sexual assault have ranged from four months to 92 years of age, rape in America has been called a tragedy of youth, with the majority of rape cases occurring during childhood and adolescence. One study reports ages of victims of forcible rapes as:
  29% less than 11 years old
  32% between the ages of 11 and 17
  22% between 18 and 24 (slightly more than one in five rapes)
  7% between 25 and 29
  6% above 29
  3% not sure or refused to answer[2]
- Most rape victims do not sustain serious physical injuries:
  70% no physical injuries
  24% minor physical injuries
  4% serious physical injuries[3]
- The most recent Uniform Crime Reports (FBI) show "unfounded" (determined false or baseless) cases of forcible rape to be slightly higher than other index crimes. The refusal of the victim to cooperate with prosecution or the failure to make an arrest does not "unfound" a legitimate offense. Also the findings of a court, jury, or prosecutor do not unfound offenses. However, if the investigation shows

[2]"Rape in America: A Report to the Nation," April 23, 1992, prepared by: National Victim Center, 2111 Wilson Boulevard, Suite 300, Arlington, Virginia 22201, and Crime Victims Research and Treatment Center, Department of Psychiatry and Behavioral Sciences, Medical University of South Carolina, Charleston, South Carolina 29425. (Percentages rounded to nearest whole number.)
[3]Ibid.

that no offense occurred nor was attempted, the reported offense can be defined unfounded.[4]

(It is this author's conclusion that with more and more victims of date and acquaintance rape reporting, the breakdown is likely to occur when investigators conclude, "It looks consensual to me." Any sexual assault center will verify that many more cases are occurring than are believed by law enforcement officials.)

- "Rape occurs far more frequently in the United States than in any other industrialized nation, according to testimony before the Senate Judiciary Committee. . . . A woman living in America is four times more likely to be raped as her counterpart in Germany, thirteen times more likely than women in England, and twenty times more likely than women in Japan."[5]
- The FBI has called forcible rape our fastest growing violent crime.
- Over two thousand organizations have emerged in the past twenty years to support rape victims.[6]

Stages of Recovery

Each person going through a crisis of any kind progresses through stages of emotional adjustment. With sexual violence, recovery may be defined various ways. Some experts classify it as "rape trauma syndrome," labeling the stages: impact, recoil, and reorganization.[7] Others term it "rape related post-traumatic stress disorder."[8]

[4]"Uniform Crime Reporting," Department of Justice, Federal Bureau of Investigation, Research and Analysis Unit.
[5]Candace Walters with Beth Spring, "The Wounds of Rape," *Christianity Today*, September 14, 1992.
[6]"Rape in America."
  The author also wishes to thank the YWCA Sexual Assault Center, Grand Rapids, Michigan, for information provided in this section.
[7]Ann Wolbert Burgess and Lynda Lytle Holmstrom, *Rape Victims of Crisis*, Bowie, Maryland: Robert J. Brady Co., 1974.
[8]"Rape Related Post-Traumatic Stress Disorder," *Infoline at a Glance*, Vol. 1, No. 38, 1992, National Victim Center, Arlington, Virginia 22201.

When I trained with my local rape crisis team, the stages below were presented as a guideline for understanding the process. Since this definition most accurately describes my own experience and has proved helpful to others, I offer it to the reader.

No time gauge can be given, since each individual and each set of circumstances is unique. A recovering victim may spend a great deal of time in one stage and only touch lightly on another. She may encounter a spiraling effect as she passes through a number of the stages over and over again, each time experiencing them with a different intensity. Or, these stages may be so clear-cut that the victim can practically assign dates to them.

Anyone close to the victim may also experience these stages as he or she adjusts to the crisis.

It is important to remember that this represents a "normal" response. In essence, *abnormal will be normal for a while, and that's okay.*

1. SHOCK — Numbness.

Any information provided to the victim during this stage will need to be repeated later, as she will most likely remember very little, if anything, about what occurs during this time.

2. DENIAL — *Not me. This can't have happened. It's not that bad. I'm fine.*

Not yet able to face the severity of the crisis, the victim spends time during this stage gathering strength. The period of denial serves as a cushion for the more difficult stages of recovery that follow.

3. ANGER — Rage, Resentment. *What did I do? Why me?*

Much of the anger may be a result of the victim's feelings of loss of strength and loss of control over her own life. The anger may be directed toward the rapist, a doctor, the police, or anyone else, including herself.

4. PLEDGE/BARGAINING — Rationalization. *Let's go on as if it didn't happen. I should be finished with it by now.*

This is a further form of denial in which the victim sets

up a bargain. She will not talk about the rape in exchange for not having to continue to experience the pain. In so doing, she continues to deny the emotional impact the rape has had upon her life. The rest of the bargain is that family and friends will also stop talking about it and pretend that it never happened.

5. DEPRESSION — Denial no longer works. *I feel so dirty . . . so worthless.*

If the victim is warned of this stage ahead of time, she may not be so thrown by it. Though a painful time for her, it is good when she reaches this stage because it shows she has begun to face the reality of the rape. As she allows her negative emotions to surface, she should be reminded that these feelings are normal and will not last forever.

She should, however, be aware of symptoms of severe depression during this stage, such as a change in sleeping or eating habits, the indulging in compulsive rituals, or generalized fears completely taking over her life. (Professional counseling is advisable.)

6. ACCEPTANCE — Life can go on.

When enough of the anger and depression is released, the victim enters the stage of acceptance. She may still spend time thinking and talking about the rape, but she understands and is in control of her own emotions and can now accept what has happened to her.

7. ASSIMILATION — The rape is put into perspective.

By the time the victim reaches this stage, she has realized her own self-worth and strength. She no longer "needs" to spend time dealing with the rape, as the total rape experience now meshes with other experiences in her life.

Common Feelings Following Sexual Violence

There may be other feelings common to recovering victims that are not listed here, and not all victims experience each of these emotions. It is important to remember that these feelings can be resolved with recovery from the crisis. (The list is presented in no particular order.)

angry
afraid
weary
sad
horrified
desperate
alone
bad
troubled
numb
unworthy
rejected
hurt
terrified
dirty
guilty
unglued
weird
hateful
worthless
unsafe
lost
shaky
fragile
confused
isolated
uptight
exhausted
betrayed
edgy
abandoned
different
bitter
damaged
burdened
defiled
overwhelmed
insecure
terrible
threatened
frustrated
uncomfortable

embarrassed
ashamed
discouraged
cold
distant
broken
weak
lifeless
empty
hopeless
scorned
helpless
unlovable
ugly
submerged
trapped
vindictive
vengeful
panic-stricken
despairing
lifeless
blamed
shamed
upset
annoyed
anxious
belittled
bottled up
crushed
depressed
desperate
miserable
despondent
envious
humiliated
inadequate
furious
incompetent
insignificant
misunderstood
nervous
put-down

regretful
relieved
resentful
shocked
disoriented
uneasy
unhappy
torn
defeated
disinterested
dissatisfied
blown away
misjudged
scared
awful
let down
rotten
mad
unprotected
tense
forgotten
alienated
hysterical
indignant
robbed
unloved
used
unwanted
forsaken
paranoid
powerless
mixed-up
violated
judged
disbelief
picked-on
unfeminine
enraged
worried
moody
crazy
foolish

impatient
dazed
criticized
distressed
grieved
detached
agitated
stressed
unsure
dependent
unacceptable
traumatized
filthy
vulnerable
shattered
grateful to be alive
want to forget
wish he had killed me
why?
I just don't understand
alone with memories
no one understands
yearn to feel normal
lacking purpose
need to escape
what's the use?
always crying
living in a prison
can't ever cry when I want to
on a roller coaster

I'll never get better
maybe it was my fault
everything's changed
not fair
no confidence
can't cope
my whole world is askew
can't trust
sick in the pit of my stomach
unbearable pain
don't know who I am anymore
full of self-contempt
self-conscious about my body
full of other-contempt
don't care how I look
can't shake it
emotionally dead
responsible for others' pain
can't concentrate
want to become invisible
want to disappear altogether
no control over what happens
    to me
want to look unattractive so no
    one will want to touch me
should have found a way to stop
    it (or prevent it)
should be finished with this by
    now

Recommended Reading

Weatherhead, Leslie D. *The Will of God* (Nashville, Tennessee: Abingdon Press, 1991).

This book helped me more than any other to resolve the questions of why God allows suffering. A timeless book, it is a series of five sermons written by a minister responding to the death and destruction of World War II. The author discusses the intentional, the circumstantial, and the ultimate will of God.

RAPE:

Ezell, Lee. *The Missing Piece* (Ann Arbor, Michigan: Servant Publications, 1992).

This is the author's own story of how she became pregnant as a result of rape, courageously gave her child up for adoption, and was reunited with her more than twenty years later. Although it focuses more on the latter elements than rape recovery, it is a powerfully moving testimony of how God replaces brokenness with healing and peace.

Lee, Susan. *The Dancer* (Grand Rapids, Michigan: Baker Book House, 1991).

This is an inspirational story of forgiveness and healing written by a recovered rape victim. Offering hope to others, Susan tells how she moved from anger and hate to sharing her testimony with women offenders through her prison dance ministry. It is quicker reading than many books on the subject.

Walters, Candace. *Invisible Wounds* (Portland, Oregon: Multnomah Press, 1992).

This is a helpful and practical resource written by a Christian rape crisis counselor and community education specialist on sexual violence, who is also a contributing editor for *Today's Christian Woman* magazine. She dispels myths and offers vital information both for the immediate aftermath and for long-term recovery. Personal accounts of victims are included.

SEXUAL ABUSE:

Allender, Dan B. *The Wounded Heart* (Colorado Springs, Colorado: NavPress, 1990).

Dr. Allender presents a thorough, comprehensive yet personal view for and about adult victims of childhood sexual abuse. He enlightens even those knowledgeable on this subject while offering hope for recovering victims. This book is a "must read" especially for Christian counselors.

Anderson, Bill. *When Child Abuse Comes to Church* (Minneapolis, Minnesota: Bethany House Publishers, 1992).

This is a pastor's account of his struggle for answers when sexual abuse impacted his own congregation. His church's trauma has been called "one of the worst, most publicized cases of multiple-child-abuse in recent history." He offers a wealth of practical information, including: detecting sexual abuse, counseling victims and their families, dealing with authorities and media, offering help to perpetrators, and much more. Reading this book causes one to plead for preventative measures on the part of every church.

Morrison, Jan. *A Safe Place* (Wheaton, Illinois: Harold Shaw Publishers, 1990).

This is written especially for teens, but provides helpful information for anyone seeking to learn more about what a victim of sexual abuse goes through. This Christian author recounts her own painful journey while presenting a cognitive look at the recovery process. Her style is personal and readable.

Heitritter, Lynn and Vought, Jeanette. *Helping Victims of Sexual Abuse* (Minneapolis, Minnesota: Bethany House Publishers, 1989).

A nine-step guide to mental, emotional, and spiritual wholeness to be used by counselors, victims, and their families.